ULTIMATE
SLOW COOKER
FAVOURITES

Cara Hobday

EBURY
PRESS

1 3 5 7 9 10 8 6 4 2

Published in 2010 by Ebury Press, an imprint of Ebury Publishing

A Random House Group Company

The Random House Group Limited Reg. No. 954009

Addresses for companies within the Random House Group can be found at www.randomhouse.co.uk

A CIP catalogue record for this book is available from the British Library

The Random House Group Limited supports The Forest Stewardship Council (FSC), the leading international forest certification organisation. All our titles that are printed on Greenpeace approved FSC certified paper carry the FSC logo. Our paper procurement policy can be found at www.rbooks.co.uk/environment

To buy books by your favourite authors and register for offers visit www.rbooks.co.uk

Colour reproduction by Dot Gradations Ltd, UK
Printed and bound in China by C & C Offset

ISBN 9780091939205

Design: Isobel Gillan
Photography: Rob White
Food styling: Cara Hobday (www.carahobday.com)
Prop styling: Luis Peral

Contents

Introduction

Whether you're already a devoted slow-cooker owner looking for new and exciting recipe ideas, or are just about to enter the world of slow cooking, this book has everything you need. We all love to come home to the aroma of our favourite meal bubbling away, and if you can throw everything into a slow cooker at the beginning of the day, no matter how late you come home you can be enjoying a hot dinner within minutes of walking through the door.

In this book you will find easy midweek suppers for all the family such as Chicken with Lemon and Garlic, or a tasty Lamb Pilaf with Tzatziki and Coriander. There are also classic comforting curries to enjoy on a Friday night, as well as stylish gastropub-style suppers which will impress your friends, including Slow-roasted Duck with Apples. For non-meat eaters there is a Meat-free Meals chapter in which you will find flavoursome vegetarian suppers such as Bolognese Pardina Lentil Sauce, which you can enjoy spooned over piping hot fresh pasta. To finish, there are even a few delicious desserts if you feel you deserve a treat after a long day!

In this collection of recipes the focus is on using economical ingredients without sacrificing flavour. I have tried to use as many storecupboard ingredients as possible, in interesting and varied combinations, to enable you to create delicious meals without having to break the bank. Here, too, you will find simpler, time-saving approaches to cooking; methods that only require you to fling all the ingredients into the pot in moments before you head out for the day.

Buying a slow cooker

When it comes to choosing the right cooker you need to decide how you intend to use it, and how many mouths you plan to feed with it. Many people find that the smallest size of slow cooker – 1.5 litres – is perfectly adequate for their needs; it is very economical to run, and ideal for making dinner for two. However, you may find that you want more from your slow cooker when you have been using it for a while.

The next size up is 3.5 litres, which is the most versatile. If you have a 4-person household, or a growing family of 2 adults and some little ones, this is probably your best bet. With this size there is room to make an ample 6 or 8 servings for dinner; or if you are cooking for fewer people you can freeze whatever isn't eaten. It also holds a whole chicken quite neatly.

For a busier household, or when there are often more than 3 or 4 for dinner, a 6.5-litre slow cooker is worth not only the investment of (not much) extra money, but the space in your kitchen, too. This has a large capacity, but don't forget that when using slow cookers the actual dishes usually only take up half the space; the extra room is for stirring and enabling the food to simmer. This larger size will happily accommodate all possible uses for the slow cooker – parties, evening meals, soups and preserves.

Energy efficiency is often a reason for buying a slow cooker, and all the modern models are very efficient. When choosing, though, look for models with more insulation and those that have a timer switch to switch the cooking mode over to 'Hold' automatically when the cooking time has ended.

Getting to grips with your slow cooker

When you first start using your slow cooker you will be surprised at how little water you need to add; this is because no moisture escapes during cooking, so all the cooking juices are kept within the dish. All the recipes in this book are tailored for slow cooking methods so they allow the right balance of liquids, but if you are adapting another recipe to cook in your slow cooker, I would recommend reducing the amount of liquid by a third initially and then add more liquid later, if needed.

For meat to remain succulent and not dry out over the long cooking times, it should be cut it into cubes of approximately 2 cm. Don't worry if the pre-cut meat that you have bought is a different size, it will still give a good result.

Many of us have now embraced slow cookers as a favoured method of cooking and wonder how we ever got by without them; we have come to rely on their comfort and convenience and see them as an invaluable resource in our kitchens. I hope that the ideas, recipes and advice in this book will help you to feel the same.

Notes on the recipes

- All vegetables are medium-sized, unless described otherwise.

- Wash all vegetables and fruit before using them.

- All diced meat should be cut into approximately 2-cm pieces.

- Salt: Maldon sea salt undoubtedly has the best flavour, without bitterness or sharpness. For this reason I think it best to use Maldon, or another sea salt, for seasoning a dish. If you also use free running table salt in your kitchen, restrict its use to salting the boiling water and reserve your Maldon for seasoning the dish.

SOUPS

spiced tomato soup

This spicy soup is made using a combination of fresh and canned tomatoes. When in season you could use all fresh, ripe fruits as this is when tomatoes are at their sweetest and most flavoursome, making this a truly spectacular soup.

serves **6** • prep time **15 mins** • cooking time **4 hours on high/8 hours on low**

6 tbsp sunflower oil
2 onions, chopped
3 carrots, chopped
2 garlic cloves, crushed
500 g very ripe tomatoes, chopped
1 tbsp paprika
1 tbsp coriander seeds, crushed
1 tbsp cumin seeds, crushed

1 tsp granulated or caster sugar
800 g canned tomatoes, chopped
300 ml hot vegetable stock
3 tbsp chopped coriander
Poppadoms, to serve
Sea salt and freshly ground
   black pepper

1 Heat half the oil in a large pan over a high heat and cook the onions, carrots and garlic for 5 minutes. Transfer to the slow cooker.

2 Heat the remaining oil in a clean pan and cook the fresh tomatoes with the paprika and the crushed coriander and cumin seeds over a medium heat for 3 minutes until it is all deliciously aromatic. Season well, then transfer to the slow cooker with the sugar.

3 Pour over the canned tomatoes and stock (you may not need all of the stock, depending on how watery the tomatoes are), then cook for 4 hours on the high setting or 8 hours on low.

4 Serve garnished with the coriander and with the poppadoms alongside.

tomato and lentil soup

A delicious twist on a classic recipe; this tasty and satisfying soup is easy to make with storecupboard ingredients. It will soon become a favourite standby; make a large quantity and you can freeze it in batches. Serve it hot with fresh crusty bread.

serves **6** • prep time **15 mins** • cooking time **4 hours on high/8 hours on low**

3 tbsp olive oil
2 onions, chopped
3 carrots, peeled and chopped
1 potato, peeled and chopped
1 bay leaf
Pinch of paprika

2 litres hot vegetable stock
2 tbsp tomato purée
500 g tomato passata
150 g red lentils
Salt and freshly ground black pepper

1 Heat the oil in a large pan over a medium heat and cook the onions, carrots and potato for 5 minutes. Transfer to the slow cooker.

2 Stir in the bay leaf and paprika, then add the stock, tomato purée, passata and lentils. Season well and cook for 4 hours on the high setting or 8 hours on low.

creamy pumpkin and lentil soup

A deliciously autumnal soup is all you need when the rain is lashing down outside and you want to warm the cockles. The addition of lentils to this hearty dish means you can simply serve some warm crusty bread alongside it to make a satisfying meal.

serves **6** • prep time **20 mins** • cooking time **4 hours on high/8 hours on low**

3 tbsp olive oil
1 kg pumpkin, peeled, seeded and
   roughly chopped
2 celery sticks, roughly chopped
2 large onions, roughly chopped
2 carrots, roughly chopped
2 garlic cloves, finely chopped

1 bay leaf
150 g red lentils
2 litres hot vegetable stock
3 tbsp crème fraîche
2 tsp sweet paprika
Salt and freshly ground black pepper

1 Heat the oil in a large pan and cook the pumpkin, celery, onions, carrots and garlic over a high heat for 10 minutes. Transfer to the slow cooker.

2 Add the bay leaf, lentils and the stock. Season well and cook for 4 hours on the high setting or 8 hours on low.

3 If you prefer a smooth soup, blend with a hand blender at this point. Check the seasoning and serve garnished with spoonfuls of crème fraîche and the paprika sprinkled over.

spiced parsnip soup

This warming wintry soup is a perennial favourite. Parsnip is a delicious and economical vegetable with a richness and full flavour that responds well to Indian spices. For an authentic touch, serve this with mini poppadoms and a bowl of cool raita alongside.

serves **6** • prep time **10 mins** • cooking time **4 hours on high/8 hours on low**

2 tbsp sunflower oil
30 g butter
2 onions, roughly chopped
1 kg parsnips, peeled and
   roughly chopped
2 garlic cloves, crushed
2 tbsp medium curry powder

1 tsp paprika (optional)
400 g can butter beans, drained
   and rinsed
1 litre hot vegetable stock
4 tbsp chopped coriander, to serve
Salt and freshly ground black pepper

1 Heat the oil and butter in a large pan and cook the onions, parsnips and garlic over a medium heat for about 5 minutes until soft. Stir in the curry powder and paprika (if using) and transfer the mixture to the slow cooker.

2 Add the beans and the stock. Season well, bring to the boil and cook for 4 hours on the high setting or 8 hours on low.

3 Blend the soup with a hand blender until smooth, check the seasoning and serve sprinkled with coriander.

hearty bean broth with herbs

Made from storecupboard ingredients, this is the perfect soup for lazy weekends when you can't face heading out to the shops. The beans hold up really well over the lengthy cooking time, so mash a few at the end to add a richness and silkiness to the texture.

serves **6** • prep time **15 mins** • cooking time **4 hours on high/8 hours on low**

50 g butter
2 celery sticks, chopped
3 carrots, chopped
2 onions, chopped
1 potato, peeled and roughly chopped
2 litres hot light vegetable stock
1 bay leaf
1 tbsp fresh or dried thyme

2 x 400 g cans haricot beans, drained
  and rinsed
2 x 400 g cans flageolet beans, drained
  and rinsed
500 g creamed tomatoes or passata
3 tbsp finely chopped flat-leaf parsley
Sea salt and freshly ground
  black pepper

1 Heat the butter in a large pan over a medium heat and lightly brown the celery, carrots and onions for 10 minutes.

2 Transfer to the slow cooker and add the potato along with the stock, bay leaf, thyme, beans and creamed tomatoes or passata. Season well then cook for 4 hours on the high setting or 8 hours on low.

3 Remove the bay leaf then take out 500 ml of the soup and blend it until smooth. Return the purée to the rest of the soup in the slow cooker and stir to blend it in. Alternatively, remove 500 ml of the soup and, using a potato masher, lightly crush the beans and return the mixture to the soup. Stir in the parsley, and serve.

SOUPS

creamy cauliflower and chickpea soup

This smooth soup is packed with goodness, despite the decadent inclusion of cream. Ideal for a sophisticated starter, or serve as a comforting lunch with warm crusty bread.

serves **6** • prep time **15 mins** • cooking time **4 hours on high/8 hours on low**

30 g butter
3 onions, chopped
1 carrot, chopped
1 cauliflower, chopped
400 g can chickpeas, drained and rinsed

500 ml hot vegetable stock
1 bay leaf
100 ml double cream
Salt and freshly ground black pepper

1 Heat the butter in a large pan over a medium heat and cook the onions and carrot for 5 minutes until softened. Transfer to the slow cooker.

2 Add the cauliflower, then the chickpeas and pour over the stock. Season well, add the bay leaf and cook for 4 hours on the high setting or 8 hours on low.

3 At the end of the cooking time, remove the bay leaf and blend the soup using a hand blender until smooth and creamy. Add cream to taste, check the seasoning, then serve immediately.

spicy tom yam thai soup

I love this spicy soup; it's guaranteed to lift the spirits and cheer you up if you're feeling under the weather. Serve it piping hot over noodles for a delicious taste sensation.

serves **6** • prep time **15 mins** • cooking time **4 hours on high/8 hours on low**

2 tbsp groundnut oil
2 onions, chopped
2 carrots, finely sliced
1 lemongrass stalk, finely chopped
2 tbsp red Thai curry paste
4 kaffir lime leaves (optional)
750 g boneless, skinless chicken breasts
   or thighs, finely diced

2 litres hot chicken stock
3 tbsp fish sauce
Cellophane rice noodles, to serve
3 spring onions, finely sliced, to serve
3 limes, quartered, to serve
Soy sauce, to serve

1 Heat half the oil in a large pan over a high heat and add the onions and carrots. Cook for 1 minute then transfer to the slow cooker. Add the lemongrass, Thai curry paste and lime leaves, if using, to the vegetables.

2 Heat the remaining oil in a large pan and cook the chicken until it is sealed all over, then transfer to the slow cooker. Pour over the stock and the fish sauce and cook for 4 hours on the high setting or 8 hours on low.

3 About 15 minutes before the end of the cooking time, add the noodles to the soup.

4 Spoon the hot soup into large bowls and sprinkle with the spring onions. (You may find it easier to use tongs to fish out the noodles, and if you prefer, a large cup is perfect to serve the broth in.) Serve with the lime quarters and the soy sauce offered separately.

chicken pot pie soup

This soup is a fantastic all-in-one lunch dish that was made famous by a London lunch bar called 'EAT'. It is just filling enough, and just warming enough not to make you sleepy for the afternoon shift.

serves **6** • prep time **15 mins** • cooking time **4 hours on high/8 hours on low**

2 tbsp sunflower oil
30 g butter
2 leeks, chopped
2 carrots, chopped
500 g boneless, skinless chicken breasts
   or thighs, finely diced
2 tbsp plain flour
300 ml hot chicken stock

300 ml milk
1 bay leaf
500 g pack ready-rolled puff pastry
1 beaten egg
100 g peas, fresh or frozen
3 tbsp finely chopped flat-leaf parsley,
Salt and freshly ground black pepper

1 Heat half the oil with all the butter in a large frying pan over a medium heat and cook the leeks and carrots for 2 minutes. Transfer everything to the slow cooker.

2 Heat the remaining oil in the frying pan over a high heat and cook the chicken until it is sealed all over. Spoon the chicken into the slow cooker and stir in the flour. Pour over the stock and milk and season well. Add the bay leaf and cook for 4 hours on the high setting or 8 hours on low.

3 To make the puff pastry 'lids', first preheat the oven to 200°C/Gas 6. Cut out 6 puff pastry rounds, each 6 cm in diameter, place them on a baking sheet and brush each with a little beaten egg. Bake in the hot oven for 10 minutes or until puffed and golden. Set aside until ready to serve. (If you are making the soup and freezing it, the uncooked pastry rounds can be frozen then baked straight from the freezer at the same temperature – simply add 5 minutes to the cooking time.)

4 About 15 minutes before the end of the cooking time, stir the peas and parsley into the soup. Serve hot in bowls topped with a puff pastry round.

sweet potato and chicken soup

This soup is the perfect revitalising all-in-one meal. I like to make it in large quantities then freeze it in portions to defrost and reheat to take to work, or for a simple supper to greet me at the end of a long day.

serves **6** • prep time **15 mins** • cooking time **4 hours on high/8 hours on low**

2 tbsp sunflower oil
30 g butter
1 leek, chopped
2 celery sticks, chopped
Few sage leaves, chopped (optional)
300 g boneless, skinless chicken
   thighs, diced

2 bay leaves
2 medium sweet potatoes, about 350 g,
   peeled and diced
1.5 litres hot chicken stock
Extra virgin olive oil, to serve
Salt and freshly ground black pepper

1 Heat the oil and butter in a large pan over a medium heat and cook the leek, celery, sage (if using) and chicken for about 3 minutes until the leeks are soft, stirring often to prevent them catching. Transfer all the ingredients to the slow cooker.

2 Add the bay leaves and sweet potatoes then pour in the stock. Season well and cook for 4 hours on the high setting or 8 hours on low.

3 If you prefer a smooth soup, blend with a hand blender at this point. (I never recommend blending hot soup in the food processor; I think it is far safer to use a stick blender in the pan.) Otherwise, simply mash with a potato masher to break down the potatoes.

4 Serve hot drizzled with extra virgin olive oil.

hungarian beef goulash soup

The ultimate meal in a bowl. This is a soupy take on the classic beef casserole dish, which makes a substantial snack or a hearty dinner for a cold day.

serves **6** • prep time **15 mins** • cooking time **4 hours on high/8 hours on low**

2 tbsp oil
30 g butter
2 onions, chopped
2 red peppers, chopped
2 green peppers, chopped
400 g beef, finely diced
1 tbsp paprika
2 tbsp tomato purée

300 ml hot beef stock
200 g tomato passata
400 g can pinto beans, drained
  and rinsed
3 tbsp finely chopped dill
6 tsp crème fraîche, to serve
Salt and freshly ground black pepper

1 Heat the oil and butter in a large frying pan over a medium heat and add the onions and peppers. Cook for 2 minutes then transfer everything to the slow cooker.

2 Add the beef, paprika, tomato purée, stock, passata and beans to the vegetables and season well. Cook for 4 hours on a high setting or 8 hours on low.

3 About 15 minutes before the end of the cooking time, stir in the dill. If you prefer a smooth soup, blend with a hand blender at this point, or serve the soup unblended, if you like a chunky texture. Serve each bowl of soup topped with a blob of crème fraîche.

LIGHT MEALS

chilli thai-style squid

Squid is a really economical seafood, and slow-cooking it brings out all its delicious flavours. A popular Mediterranean and Eastern ingredient, squid is the perfect partner to all kinds of spices, and its natural richness means it needs little else to make this a simple yet satisfying curry.

 serves **6** • prep time **20 mins** • cooking time **4 hours on high/8 hours on low**

3 tbsp vegetable or olive oil
1 kg frozen squid, diced
4 spring onions, sliced
3 garlic cloves, sliced
2 carrots, sliced
90 g red Thai curry paste
3 tbsp Thai fish sauce
440 ml coconut milk

2 tbsp soy sauce
1 red pepper, chopped
6 tbsp fresh lime juice
2 tbsp finely chopped coriander leaves
2 tbsp finely chopped basil leaves
1 red chilli, seeded and finely sliced
Thai jasmine rice, to serve

1 Heat the oil in a frying pan over a high heat and cook the squid, spring onions, garlic and carrots for 2 minutes until lightly browned. Transfer to the slow cooker.

2 In the frying pan, combine the curry paste with the fish sauce, coconut milk and soy sauce. Heat to a simmer and pour over the squid. Add the red pepper to the curry and cook for 4 hours on the high setting or 8 hours on low.

3 Just before serving, cook the rice according to the packet instructions.

4 Add the lime juice, coriander, basil and chilli to the curry, mix it in well and serve in large bowls with the rice.

squid pilaf with parsley and garlic

You can buy squid ready-prepared in most supermarkets, but if you're lucky enough to have a fishmonger near you, ask him to cut up a fresh squid for you. Squid can be quite rich, but in this recipe its flavour is kept fresh with the addition of spring onions.

serves **6** • prep time **15 mins** • cooking time **3 hours on high/6 hours on low**

2 tbsp olive oil
400 g squid tubes, sliced into rings
1 large mild onion, chopped
2 carrots, chopped
1 bay leaf
2 tsp coriander seeds, crushed
1 tsp chilli flakes
3 garlic cloves, chopped

200 g brown rice, washed
200 g puy lentils, washed
1 litre hot fish stock
50 g flat-leaf parsley, chopped
6 spring onions, finely sliced
Rocket salad, to serve
Salt and freshly ground black pepper

1 Heat the oil in a large frying pan over a medium heat. Add the squid rings, onion and carrots and fry for a couple of minutes until golden. Transfer to the slow cooker.

2 Add the bay leaf, coriander seeds, chilli flakes and garlic and fry gently until the spices are aromatic.

3 Stir in the rice and lentils, pour on the stock and cook for 3 hours on the high setting or 6 hours on low.

4 Just before serving, stir through the parsley and spring onions. Serve hot with the rocket salad.

seafood risotto

You may find your local supermarket or deli has a variety of risotto rices on offer, including the most commonly available Arborio and Carnaroli varieties. However, for slow cooking I would recommend using the equally widely sold *Vialone nano*, because even after lengthy cooking it keeps some texture and the essential 'bite' that is needed for the perfect risotto.

serves **6** • prep time **15 mins** • cooking time **4 hours on high/8 hours on low**

2 tbsp olive oil
2 onions, chopped
3 garlic cloves, chopped
500 g vialone nano risotto rice
1 bay leaf
1 tsp paprika
250 ml white wine

1 litre hot fish stock
500 ml shellfish soup
400 g frozen seafood, defrosted
100 g grated Parmesan
12 cherry tomatoes, halved
Salt and freshly ground black pepper

1 Heat the oil in a large pan over a medium heat and cook the onions and garlic for about 10 minutes until soft but not coloured.

2 Add the rice, bay leaf, paprika and wine and cook for a few minutes to heat it all through.

3 Transfer everything to the slow cooker and add the stock, shellfish soup and seafood. Season well and cook for 4 hours on the high setting or 8 hours on low.

4 Stir through the Parmesan and the cherry tomatoes before serving.

crayfish pilaf with fresh rocket salsa

Crayfish are now widely available in the freezer cabinet of most super-markets, and their meaty succulence makes a nice change from prawns and other shellfish traditionally used in pilaf. This recipe uses brown rice in combination with spelt grain, which is a healthy wholegrain with a low gluten content, so it's good to serve to someone who is gluten intolerant.

serves **6** • prep time **15 mins** • cooking time **3 hours on high/6 hours on low**

3 tbsp olive oil
1 large mild onion, chopped
3 garlic cloves, chopped
1 bay leaf
150 g brown rice, washed
150 g spelt grain, washed
1.2 litres hot fish stock
300 g raw king prawns, peeled
350 g frozen cooked crayfish, defrosted
   and halved

85 g bag rocket and watercress salad
2 tbsp flat-leaf parsley
3 spring onions, finely sliced
2 tomatoes, chopped
1 fresh red chilli, seeded and finely
   chopped (optional)
Sea salt and freshly ground
   black pepper

1 Heat 2 tablespoons of the oil in a large frying pan over a medium heat. Add the onion and garlic and fry for 3–4 minutes until the onion is softened. Stir in the bay leaf, rice and spelt and mix to coat in the oil. Transfer everything to the slow cooker.

2 Pour over the stock and stir in the prawns. Cook for 3 hours on the high setting or 6 hours on low.

3 About 30 minutes before the end of the cooking time, stir in the crayfish.

4 To make the salsa, blend together the rocket salad, parsley, spring onions, tomatoes, chilli (if using) and remaining oil in a food processor or blender until finely chopped. Season well.

5 Serve the crayfish pilaf with the rocket salsa on the side.

tuna baked with artichokes and capers

This is one of my favourite dishes, and one I can eat all year round as many of the ingredients are good storecupboard standbys. Fish and capers are a classic combination, and here mildly flavoured tuna is given a real lift from the slightly bitter artichokes and salty capers. For the best result, cook on high for the shorter time.

 serves **4** • prep time**15 mins** • cooking time **4 hours on high/8 hours on low**

2 tbsp olive oil
4 tuna steaks, approx. 125 g each
3 garlic cloves, crushed
Grated zest of 1 lemon
2 tbsp salted capers, drained and rinsed

4 tbsp finely chopped flat-leaf parsley
200 ml white wine
100 ml hot fish stock
280 g jar artichokes in oil, drained
Salt and freshly ground black pepper

1   Heat the oil in a large frying pan over a high heat and fry the tuna steaks for about a minute on each side until golden. Transfer to the slow cooker.

2   Add the garlic, lemon zest, capers and parsley to the slow cooker. Pour over the wine and stock and season well. Cook for 4 hours on the high setting or 8 hours on low.

3   About 15 minutes before the end of the cooking time, add the artichokes. Serve piping hot.

tuna and spinach hotpot

Some light meals can leave those with a hearty appetite still feeling hungry, however tuna steaks are always satisfying – even for the most committed carnivore! If you're not confident at cooking tuna, slow cooking is the answer, as you are not at risk of overcooking the fish and leaving it dry. Make sure the pan is quite hot before you add the tuna so that the golden crust forms quickly. Serve with hot boiled new potatoes.

serves **4** • prep time **15 mins** • cooking time **4 hours on high/8 hours on low**

2 tbsp olive oil
4 x 150 g tuna steaks
2 garlic cloves, crushed
400 g can chopped tomatoes
100 ml white wine
200 g spinach leaves, washed and
   roughly chopped

4 tbsp finely chopped flat-leaf parsley
   to serve
Sea salt and freshly ground
   black pepper

1 Heat the oil in a large frying pan over a high heat. Season the tuna steaks and cook for 3 minutes or until golden. Add the garlic for the last minute. Transfer everything to the slow cooker, with all the pan juices.

2 Add the tomatoes and wine to the slow cooker and season well, then cook for 4 hours on the high setting or 8 hours on low.

3 About 10 minutes before the end of the cooking time, stir in the spinach leaves. Serve garnished with the parsley.

mediterranean swordfish and olive stew

This tasty dish has all the flavours of the Mediterranean; one mouthful will transport you there in an instant. This low-fat, full-flavoured stew makes an easy, light midweek supper or a simple yet impressive dinner-party dish.

serves **4** • prep time **15 mins** • cooking time **4 hours on high/8 hours on low**

2 tbsp olive oil
2 onions, chopped
1 carrot, chopped
1 red pepper, chopped
3 garlic cloves, crushed
1 tbsp fennel seeds
400 g can chopped tomatoes

4 x 150 g swordfish steaks
200 ml white wine
Grated zest of 1 lemon
4 tbsp finely chopped flat-leaf parsley
100 g black olives, pitted and chopped
Sea salt and freshly ground
    black pepper

1 Heat half the oil in a medium frying pan over a medium heat and cook the onions, carrot, pepper and garlic for 2 minutes until soft. Transfer to the slow cooker and stir in the fennel seeds and tomatoes.

2 Heat the remaining oil in a large clean frying pan over a high heat. Season the swordfish steaks and cook them for 1 minute on each side. Add the cooked fish to the slow cooker.

3 Add the wine to the hot frying pan, simmer for a couple of minutes to burn off the alcohol, then pour the liquid into the slow cooker. Cook the stew for 4 hours on the high setting or 8 hours on low.

4 Mix together the lemon zest, parsley and black olives and sprinkle over the stew to serve.

chicken with sweet and sour noodles

This is a great dish for all the family, and a particular favourite of hungry children returning from school. For a more substantial meal, serve it with spring rolls and sesame toasts.

serves **6** • prep time **15 mins** • cooking time **4 hours on high/8 hours on low**

900 g boneless skinless chicken thighs
2 tbsp cornflour
4 tbsp soy sauce
4 tbsp granulated or caster sugar
100 ml garlic vinegar
6 tbsp tomato purée
100 ml orange juice
225 g can pineapple in natural juice
200 ml hot chicken stock

2 tbsp groundnut oil
2 onions, sliced
1 red pepper, roughly chopped
1 green pepper, roughly chopped
2 carrots, sliced
Rice noodles, to serve
Salt and freshly ground black pepper

1 Season the chicken and toss it in the cornflour to coat.

2 In a bowl, mix together the soy sauce, sugar, vinegar, tomato purée, orange juice, pineapple and stock and pour everything into the slow cooker.

3 Heat the oil in a large frying pan over a medium heat and cook the onions, peppers and carrots for 2 minutes. When just golden, transfer to the slow cooker. Season.

4 Add the chicken to the other ingredients in the slow cooker and cook for 4 hours on the high setting or 8 hours on low.

5 About 15 minutes before serving, cook the rice noodles: drop the noodles into a large pan of boiling water, and when it returns to the boil, add a cup of cold water. Repeat this, then when the water boils for the third time, drain the noodles, which will be cooked perfectly.

6 Scoop out the cooked chicken from the slow cooker and serve with the noodles stirred into the sweet and sour sauce.

chicken with artichokes and pink peppercorns

This may not seem an obvious combination of ingredients, but pink peppercorns have a fragrant flavour and a lovely texture that marry surprisingly well with slightly bitter artichokes. Serve with fresh pasta for a delicious and impressive dinner-party dish.

serves **6** • prep time **15 mins** • cooking time **4 hours on high/8 hours on low**

1.5 kg chicken pieces, skin removed
2 tbsp olive oil
1 tbsp plain flour
2 mild onions, chopped
2 red peppers, chopped
4 garlic cloves, chopped
2 tbsp pink peppercorns in brine,
   drained

100 ml white wine
280 g jar artichokes in brine, drained
Tagliatelle, to serve
4 tbsp chopped flat-leaf parsley,
   to serve
Salt and freshly ground black pepper

1 Season the chicken. Heat half the oil in a large frying pan over a medium heat and fry the chicken until golden all over. Spoon into the slow cooker and stir in the flour.

2 Heat the remaining oil in the pan and soften the onions, peppers and garlic. Add to the slow cooker. Crush the peppercorns lightly and add to the slow cooker. Stir in the white wine, spoon the artichokes on top and cook for 4 hours on the high setting or 8 hours on low.

3 Towards the end of the cooking time, cook the tagliatelle according to the packet instructions. Sprinkle the parsley over before serving. Drain, then serve immediately with the chicken and sauce.

chicken with beans, hazelnuts and orange

I love to add lots of texture and flavour to a dish in place of richness. Crunchy hazelnuts, tangy oranges and succulent green beans make this a tasty dish.

serves **6** • prep time **15 mins** • cooking time **4 hours on high/8 hours on low**

1.5 kg chicken pieces, skin removed	100 ml hot chicken stock
2 tbsp olive oil	100 ml fresh orange juice
1 tbsp plain flour	200 g green beans, halved
6 shallots, roughly sliced	4 tbsp chopped flat-leaf parsley
3 garlic cloves, chopped	1 kg new potatoes, to serve
50 g hazelnuts, halved	Salt and freshly ground black pepper

1 Season the chicken. Heat half the oil in a large frying pan over a medium heat and fry the chicken until golden all over. Spoon into the slow cooker and stir in the flour.

2 Heat the remaining oil in the frying pan and soften the shallots and garlic. Add to the slow cooker with the hazelnuts, stock and orange juice and cook for 4 hours on the high setting or 8 hours on low.

3 About 30 minutes before the end of cooking time, add the beans and stir in the parsley.

4 Towards the end of the cooking time, cook the new potatoes over a high heat in a pan of lightly salted boiling water until tender. Serve immediately with the chicken and sauce.

turkey with black olives, tomatoes and basil

Turkey makes a good low-fat alternative to chicken and tastes delicious in this traditional Italian sauce of olives, tomatoes and basil. For a truly authentic meal, serve it with your favourite fresh pasta.

serves **4** • prep time **15 mins** • cooking time **4 hours on high/8 hours on low**

4 turkey breast steaks, approx.
  500 g in total
2 tbsp olive oil
2 onions, roughly chopped
1 carrot, chopped
2 garlic cloves, left whole

100 g pitted black olives, sliced
1 tbsp tomato purée
500 g tomato passata
15g basil leaves, to serve
Sea salt and freshly ground
  black pepper

1 Season the turkey steaks. Heat half the oil in a large frying pan over a high heat and brown the steaks on both sides. Transfer to the slow cooker.

2 Heat the remaining oil in the frying pan and cook the onions, carrot and garlic over a medium heat for 5 minutes. Add to the slow cooker.

3 Stir in the tomato purée, passata and seasoning and cook for 4 hours on the high setting or 8 hours on low. Garnish with basil before serving.

harissa turkey stew

This light yet satisfying dish is inspired by North African cuisine; it has a real kick thanks to the fiery and vibrant harissa paste. Plain couscous makes the perfect accompaniment to this flavoursome stew.

serves **4** • prep time **15 mins** • cooking time **4 hours on high/8 hours on low**

4 turkey breast steaks, approx.
    500 g in total
2 tbsp oil
2 red onions, roughly chopped
2 carrots, peeled and roughly chopped
4 garlic cloves, left whole
1 lemon, rinsed and roughly chopped
1 tbsp tomato purée

250 g tomato passata
1 cinnamon stick
4 tbsp chopped coriander leaves
300 g couscous, to serve
Harissa paste, to taste
Natural yoghurt, to serve
Sea salt and freshly ground
    black pepper

1 Season the turkey steaks. Heat half the oil in a large frying pan over a high heat and brown the turkey steaks on both sides. Transfer to the slow cooker.

2 Heat the remaining oil in the frying pan and cook the onions, carrots and garlic in over a medium heat for 5 minutes. Add to the slow cooker with the lemon pieces.

3 Stir in the tomato purée, passata, cinnamon and seasoning and cook for 4 hours on the high setting or 8 hours on low.

4 Just before serving, prepare the couscous according to the packet instructions. Stir the coriander into the stew and serve hot over the couscous with some harissa paste and yoghurt in separate bowls to be passed around.

turkey meatballs with red pepper sauce

If you're not a fan of onions, this recipe is for you. Onion-free, the dish instead derives flavour from its lovely rich red pepper sauce.

serves **4** • prep time **15 mins** • cooking time **4 hours on high/8 hours on low**

400 g turkey mince
1 egg white
290 g jar red peppers in brine, drained
500 g tomato passata
2 tbsp oil
2 garlic cloves, crushed
? tsp cayenne pepper

400 g can cannellini beans, drained and rinsed
1 large sprig of thyme leaves, chopped
600 g spaghetti, to serve
Green salad, to serve
Salt and freshly ground black pepper

1 Season the mince and stir in the egg white to bind. Divide the mix into 12 pieces and roll in your hands to form 12 meatballs.

2 Blend the red peppers and passata together in a blender or food processor until well combined. Season.

3 Heat the oil in a large frying pan over a high heat and cook the meatballs for about 2 minutes until just brown all over. Add the garlic for the second minute then transfer everything to the slow cooker.

4 Add the blended red peppers to the slow cooker with the cayenne, beans and thyme and cook for 4 hours on the high setting or 8 hours on low.

5 Just before serving, cook the spaghetti according to the packet instructions. Drain and serve with the meatballs and sauce, with a green salad on the side.

EASY MIDWEEK
SUPPERS

chicken with leeks, bacon and mustard

This tasty chicken casserole is a real crowd-pleaser and so versatile. A meal for any occasion, it can welcome you home at the end of a long day, or makes a delicious hassle-free weekend lunch for friends.

serves **6** • prep time **15 mins** • cooking time **4 hours on high/8 hours on low**

2 tbsp plain flour
1.5 kg chicken pieces
4 tbsp oil
100 g streaky bacon, diced
2 leeks, finely chopped
2 bay leaves
2 tbsp wholegrain Dijon mustard

2 tsp mustard powder
300 ml hot chicken stock
Salt and freshly ground black pepper
2.5 kg Maris Piper potatoes, peeled
   and chopped
50 g butter
100 ml milk

1 Season the flour with salt and pepper, then toss the chicken pieces in the flour, coating thoroughly.

2 Heat half the oil in a large frying pan over a high heat, add the chicken and cook for about 5 minutes until browned. Transfer to the slow cooker.

3 Heat the remaining oil in the pan over a medium heat and add the bacon and leeks. Cook for about 5 minutes until softened. Stir in the bay leaves and both mustards and transfer everything to the slow cooker. Add the stock and cook for 4 hours on the high setting or 8 hours on low.

4 To make the mashed potato, 30 minutes before serving put the potatoes in a large pan with enough cold salted water to cover. Bring to the boil then cook, uncovered, for 15 minutes or until tender, then drain well. Return the potatoes to the pan with the butter and milk and season well. Mash with a potato masher for some texture, or use a potato ricer or food mill if you prefer a smoother version.

5 Serve the chicken on top of the mashed potato with the sauce poured over.

piquant chicken with red and yellow peppers

This simple supper is guaranteed to lift the spirits on a week night. To save time, I have used red peppers from a jar rather than roasting them myself. Be sure to drain them well, though, so that you only get the flavour of the peppers, not the brine.

serves **6** • prep time **15 mins** • cooking time **4 hours on high/8 hours on low**

1.5 kg chicken pieces
4 tbsp olive oil
1 tbsp plain flour
2 yellow peppers, chopped
2 onions, chopped
2 garlic cloves, crushed
2 flamed red peppers in brine, chopped

3 tbsp tomato purée
1 bay leaf
1 tbsp paprika
2 tbsp balsamic vinegar
300 g long grain rice, to serve
Salt and freshly ground black pepper

1 Season the chicken. Heat half the oil in a large frying pan over a high heat and cook the chicken until browned. Transfer to the slow cooker and stir in the flour.

2 Heat the remaining oil in the frying pan and soften the yellow peppers, onions and garlic over a medium heat for 5 minutes. Season and stir in the tomato purée, red peppers, and bay leaf. Spoon everything into the slow cooker.

3 Stir in the paprika and balsamic vinegar and cook for 4 hours on the high setting or 8 hours on low.

4 Just before serving, cook the rice according to the packet instructions. Serve the chicken spooned over the cooked rice.

chicken korma

Chicken korma is a rich and mild curry, which makes it ideal for serving as a family dinner or to a crowd of friends with varying tastes. For those who do prefer a bit of heat in their curry, serve it with a spicy condiment such as a chilli relish.

serves **6** • prep time **20 mins** • cooking time **4 hours on high/8 hours on low**

4 tbsp butter
1.8 kg chicken pieces
2 onions, sliced
4 garlic cloves, crushed
5 cm piece of fresh root ginger,
   finely grated
50 g korma curry paste

3 tbsp tomato purée
300 ml hot chicken stock
200 ml coconut milk
15 g coriander, chopped
350 g basmati rice, to serve
50 g flaked almonds, toasted, to serve
Salt and freshly ground black pepper

1 Heat half the butter in a large frying pan set over a high heat. Season the chicken pieces and brown them all over. You will probably have to do this in batches. Transfer to the slow cooker.

2 Heat the remaining butter in the frying pan and brown the onions over a high heat, then stir in the garlic, ginger and curry paste. Transfer to the slow cooker and add the tomato purée, stock and coconut milk, stirring well. Season and cook for 4 hours on the high setting or 8 hours on low.

3 Just before serving, cook the rice according to the packet instructions. Stir the coriander into the curry and serve piping hot over the rice, garnished with the almonds.

chicken with lemon and garlic

This simple combination is delicious as an al fresco dish. Served with a green vegetable and fried potatoes, you will be transported to a French summer with every mouthful.

serves **6** • prep time **15 mins** • cooking time **4 hours on high/8 hours on low**

6 tbsp olive oil
1.5 kg chicken pieces
3 lemons, sliced
2 onions, chopped
6 garlic cloves, halved
100 ml white wine

100 ml hot chicken stock
4 tbsp chopped flat-leaf parsley,
   to serve
Green beans, to serve
Salt and freshly ground black pepper

1 Heat half the oil in a large frying pan over a medium heat. Fry the chicken until golden all over, season well and spoon into the slow cooker.

2 Heat the remaining oil in the frying pan and cook the lemons, onions and garlic over a medium heat for 5 minutes until softened. Transfer to the slow cooker.

3 Stir in the wine and stock, season well and cook for 4 hours on the high setting or 8 hours on low. Stir in the parsley just before serving.

warming chicken casserole

Chicken is such a versatile family food and so easy to prepare. This traditional casserole will win a place in your repertoire for its simple comforting flavours. It's perfect for serving with a mound of creamy mashed potato.

serves **6** • prep time **15 mins** • cooking time **4 hours on high/8 hours on low**

1.5 kg chicken pieces
50 g butter
100 g streaky bacon, each rasher
   cut into 3
2 tbsp plain flour
2 onions, chopped

3 carrots, chopped
2 celery sticks, chopped
2 bay leaves
100 ml hot chicken stock
1 tbsp Dijon mustard
Salt and freshly ground black pepper

1 Season the chicken pieces. Heat half the butter in a large frying pan over a medium heat and brown the chicken and bacon. Transfer to the slow cooker and stir in the flour.

2 Heat the remaining butter in the frying pan and soften the onions, carrots and celery. Transfer everything to the slow cooker.

3 Add the bay leaves, stock and mustard. Season well and cook for 4 hours on the high setting or 8 hours on low.

chicken pasta sauce
with sweet potato and rosemary

Sometimes a more hearty pasta sauce is needed on a cold winter evening. This sauce has all the texture of the sweet potato and the flavour of the rosemary for the pasta to soak up. Serve with lots of freshly grated Parmesan.

serves **4** • prep time **15 mins** • cooking time **4 hours on high/8 hours on low**

400 g boneless, skinless chicken thighs, diced
3 tbsp olive oil
2 garlic cloves
2 tbsp finely chopped rosemary
400 g sweet potatoes, peeled and chopped

2 leeks, chopped
200 ml hot chicken stock
100 ml crème fraîche
300 g tagliatelle, to serve
4 tbsp finely chopped flat-leaf parsley
Salt and freshly ground black pepper

1 Season the chicken. Heat half the oil in a large frying pan over a medium heat. Fry the chicken until golden all over then transfer to the slow cooker.

2 Chop together the garlic and rosemary with a bit of salt. Heat the remaining oil in the frying pan and soften the sweet potatoes, leeks and rosemary and garlic. Transfer to the slow cooker.

3 Add the stock, season, and cook for 4 hours on the high setting or 8 hours on low.

4 Just before serving, cook the pasta according to the packet instructions and stir the crème fraîche into the sauce.

5 Serve hot spooned over the tagliatelle and garnished with the parsley.

curried duck with pineapple

Duck lends itself beautifully to fruity flavours, and in this recipe the sweetness of the pineapple is the perfect complement to the spices. Serve with a zesty lime pickle if you want a little extra zing.

serves **6** • prep time **15 mins** • cooking time **4 hours on high/8 hours on low**

6 duck legs, excess fat removed
1 tbsp oil
2 onions, chopped
3 garlic cloves, crushed
5 cm piece of fresh root ginger, grated
1 tsp cayenne pepper
1 tsp ground turmeric
1 tbsp coriander seeds, crushed
1 tbsp cumin seeds, crushed

1 tbsp tomato purée
450 g can pineapple slices in
   juice, drained
1 red chilli, seeded and chopped
100 ml hot chicken stock
350 g basmati rice, to serve
Lime pickle, to serve
Salt and freshly ground black pepper

1   Season the duck legs then fry them in a large dry frying pan over a high heat. Drain on kitchen paper then place them in the slow cooker.

2   Drain off any excess fat from the frying pan, add the oil and place over a medium heat to cook the onions, garlic and ginger together for 5 minutes until softened. Stir in the cayenne, turmeric, coriander and cumin seeds and tomato purée. Transfer to the slow cooker with the pineapple, chilli and stock. Season and cook for 4 hours on the high setting or 8 hours on low.

3   Just before serving, cook the rice according to the packet instructions. Spoon off any excess fat from the duck (you may also want to take the meat off the bone, if time allows) and serve hot with lime pickle and the rice.

coconut and coriander lamb curry

This lamb curry will be a hit with all the family; it is mild but it has a variety of flavours that will suit even the most discerning palate. If you prefer a hotter curry, add a little chopped fresh chilli – enough to add some heat but not overpower it.

serves **6** • prep time **20 mins** • cooking time **4 hours on high/8 hours on low**

2 tbsp oil
1.2 kg lamb shoulder, diced
3 onions, chopped
4 garlic cloves, chopped
1 tbsp grated fresh root ginger
1 tbsp coriander seeds, crushed
4 cardamom pods, crushed

1 tbsp ground turmeric
1 tbsp chilli flakes
150 g coconut cream
300 ml hot lamb stock
400 g low-fat natural yoghurt
4 tbsp chopped coriander
350 g basmati rice, to serve

1 Heat half the oil in a large frying pan over a high heat and brown the lamb well all over. Transfer to the slow cooker.

2 Heat the remaining oil in the frying pan over a medium heat and stir in the onions, garlic, ginger, coriander seeds, cardamom, turmeric and chilli flakes until aromatic. Add to the slow cooker with the coconut cream, stock and yoghurt and cook for 4 hours on the high setting or 8 hours on low.

3 About 20 minutes before the end of the cooking time, add the coriander and cook the basmati rice according to the packet instructions.

4 Serve hot over the rice.

lamb pilaf with tzatziki and coriander

I love to serve tzatziki or houmous, if you prefer, with pilaf; they add a fresh flavour, and a creamy dimension to the texture of the dish.

serves **6** • prep time **15 mins** • cooking time **3 hours on high/6 hours on low**

6 tbsp olive oil
1 large mild onion, chopped
2 carrots, chopped
1 bay leaf
1 tbsp coriander seeds, crushed
1 tbsp cumin seeds
3 garlic cloves, chopped
500 g lamb shoulder, diced

250 g brown rice, washed
800 ml lamb stock
50 g coriander, chopped
4 tomatoes, chopped
6 spring onions, finely sliced
150 g tzatziki
6 lemon wedges

1 Heat half the oil in a large frying pan over a medium heat. Add the onion, carrots, bay leaf, coriander seeds, cumin seeds and garlic and fry for 3–4 minutes until the spices are aromatic and the onion is softened. Transfer to the slow cooker.

2 Heat the remaining oil in the frying pan and brown the lamb all over. Stir in the rice and coat it in the oil. Transfer to the slow cooker.

3 Pour over the stock and cook for 3 hours on the high setting or 6 hours on low.

4 At the end of the cooking time, mix together the coriander, tomatoes and spring onions in a bowl to make a salsa. Serve the pilaf with the salsa and tzatziki on the side, with some lemon wedges.

lamb with apricots and couscous

Couscous makes a fantastic speedy midweek meal and it perfectly offsets this lamb dish, which is packed with goodness. Lamb, apricot and spices are a classic North African combination, and the aroma of this cooking will make you feel as if you're in warmer climes!

serves **6** • prep time **15 mins** • cooking time **4 hours on high/8 hours on low**

800 g lean diced lamb
3 tbsp olive oil
2 mild onions, chopped
2 carrots, chopped
1 waxy potato, peeled and diced
1 tbsp paprika
3 cm piece cinnamon stick
1 tbsp fennel seeds
4 garlic cloves, left whole

1 bay leaf
500 ml hot chicken stock
400 g couscous
150 g dried apricots, soaked and halved, or ready-to-eat apricots, halved
4 tbsp chopped coriander, to serve
Natural yoghurt, to serve
Salt and freshly ground black pepper

1 Season the lamb. Heat 2 tablespoons of the oil in a large frying pan over a high heat. Brown the lamb, in batches if necessary, and spoon into the slow cooker.

2 Heat the remaining oil in the frying pan and brown the onions, carrots and potato. Stir in the paprika, cinnamon and fennel seeds, then transfer everything to the slow cooker. Season well.

3 Add the garlic, bay leaf and stock and cook for 4 hours on the high setting or 8 hours on low.

4 About 30 minutes before the end of the cooking time, pour boiling water over the couscous and leave to stand for 10 minutes. Mix together the couscous and apricots and spoon it over the surface of the tagine. Replace the lid and let the couscous steam until tender.

5 Serve with the couscous sprinkled with coriander, and the yoghurt handed round separately.

lamb and cauliflower kashmir curry

Middle-neck lamb chops are perfect for slow cooking as they need to be cooked out for a length of time to tenderise and for their full flavour to be released. The bone means that the chops hold together well during cooking and also remain succulent.

serves **6–8** • prep time **15 mins** • cooking time **4 hours on high/8 hours on low**

1 kg middle-neck lamb chops
4 tbsp oil
3 onions, sliced
4 garlic cloves, chopped
250 g cauliflower in florets
50 g Kashmiri curry paste
1 tbsp ground turmeric

100 g whole almonds
200 ml hot lamb stock
300 ml natural low-fat yoghurt
2 tsp cornflour
350 g basmati rice, 1 cardamom pod
    and 1 bay leaf, to serve
Salt and freshly ground black pepper

1 Season the meat. Heat half the oil in a large frying pan over a high heat and brown the chops on both sides. Add them to the slow cooker.

2 Heat the remaining oil in the frying pan and cook the onions and garlic for about 5 minutes over a medium heat until well softened. Add the cauliflower for the last 2 minutes then transfer everything to the slow cooker.

3 Stir in the curry paste, turmeric, almonds and stock. In a bowl, mix together the yoghurt and cornflour and add this to the slow cooker. Cook for 4 hours on the high setting or 8 hours on low.

4 Just before serving, cook the basmati rice according to the packet instructions, adding the cardamom pod and bay leaf to the pan. Serve the hot curry over the flavoured basmati rice.

lamb and chickpea moroccan stew

Stews like this one are perfect in the slow cooker – economical, tasty and requiring minimum preparation. It's the perfect restorative supper dish after a long day at work or school.

serves: **6** • prep time **15 mins** • cooking time **4 hours on high/8 hours on low**

800 g lean diced lamb
3 tbsp olive oil
2 onions, chopped
3 carrots, chopped
3 celery sticks, chopped
1 tbsp coriander seeds, crushed
1 tbsp cumin seeds
1 tbsp ground cinnamon
4 garlic cloves, left whole

400 g can chickpeas, drained
500 ml hot chicken stock
400 g can chopped tomatoes, or 450 g
    fresh tomatoes, roughly chopped
600 g couscous
Salt and freshly ground black pepper
Lemon wedges, harissa paste and
    natural yoghurt

1 Season the lamb. Heat 2 tablespoons of the oil in a large frying pan over a high heat. Brown the lamb, in batches if necessary, and spoon into the slow cooker.

2 Heat the remaining oil in the frying pan and brown the onions, carrots and celery over a medium heat for 5 minutes. Add the coriander seeds, cumin seeds, cinnamon and garlic and transfer everything to the slow cooker.

3 Stir in the chickpeas, stock and tomatoes and season well. Cook for 4 hours on the high setting or 8 hours on low.

4 About 30 minutes before the end of the cooking time, pour boiling water over the couscous and leave to stand for 10 minutes. Spoon the soaked couscous over the surface of the stew, replace the lid and let the couscous steam for the remaining cooking time.

5 Serve the stew with the couscous, and with the lemon wedges, harissa and yoghurt handed round separately.

hearty pork casserole with apples

A classic combination that evokes the aromas and flavours of autumn. The sharpness of the apples cuts through the pork beautifully.

serves **6** • prep time **20 mins** • cooking time **4 hours on high/8 hours on low**

1.2 kg pork shoulder, diced
2 tbsp olive oil
2 leeks, roughly chopped
1 turnip, roughly chopped
1 celery stick, roughly chopped
2 Granny Smith apples, cored and chopped
200 g streaky bacon, each rasher cut into 3
3 tbsp dried mixed herbs

1 bay leaf
100 ml cider
300 ml hot chicken stock
1 tbsp black treacle
2 tsp mustard powder
$\frac{1}{2}$ Savoy cabbage, shredded
2.5 kg Maris Piper potatoes, chopped
50 g butter
100 ml milk
Salt and freshly ground black pepper

1 Season the pork. Heat half the oil in a large frying pan over a high heat and brown the pork, in batches if necessary. Transfer to the slow cooker.

2 Heat the remaining oil and cook the leeks, turnip, celery, apples and bacon over a high heat, stirring for approximately 5 minutes, until golden. Spoon into the slow cooker and stir in the mixed herbs with the bay leaf.

3 Add the cider, stock, black treacle and mustard powder, mix well, season, and cook for 4 hours on the high setting or 8 hours on low.

4 To make the mashed potato, 30 minutes before serving put the potatoes in a pan with enough cold salted water to cover. Bring to the boil then cook, uncovered, for 15 minutes or until tender, then drain. Return the potatoes to the pan with the butter and milk and season well. Mash with a potato masher for some texture, or use a potato ricer or food mill if you prefer a smoother version.

5 About 15 minutes before the end of the cooking time, stir the cabbage into the casserole. Serve piping hot with the mashed potato.

curried rabbit casserole

Rabbit's firm, meaty flesh is excellent for casseroles and stews, and its strong flavour works particularly well in a curry. This is not too spicy for children and those with sensitive palates, but if you prefer more heat, increase the cayenne content to taste.

serves **4** • prep time **15 mins** • cooking time **4 hours on high/8 hours on low**

1 kg rabbit pieces, or
   1 whole rabbit, jointed
4 tbsp oil
4 garlic cloves, crushed
2 onions, chopped
2 carrots, diced
2 tbsp medium curry powder

1 tsp cayenne pepper (optional)
1 bay leaf
200 ml hot chicken stock
250 g basmati rice, to serve
4 tbsp crème fraîche
Mango chutney, to serve
Salt and freshly ground black pepper

1 Season the rabbit. Heat half the oil in a large frying pan over a high heat and brown the meat well. Transfer to the slow cooker.

2 Heat the remaining oil and soften the garlic, onions and carrots over a medium heat. Stir in the curry powder, cayenne (if using) and the bay leaf. Transfer everything to the slow cooker.

3 Deglaze the pan with a little of the stock and add to the slow cooker with the rest of the stock. Season well then cook for 4 hours on the high setting or 8 hours on low.

4 Just before serving, cook the rice according to the packet instructions and stir the crème fraîche into the rabbit casserole. Serve with the rice and a dollop of mango chutney.

game casserole with winter vegetables

Game is fast becoming popular as an alternative to the more traditional chicken. It is widely available in supermarkets, generally between August and February when it comes into season, and is the ultimate organic meat.

serves **6** • prep time **15 mins** • cooking time **4 hours on high/8 hours on low**

800 g mixed game pack, diced
4 tbsp butter
1 tbsp plain flour
2 onions, chopped
2 carrots, diced
½ a celeriac, peeled and diced
3 small turnips, peeled and quartered
300 ml hot game stock

1 bay leaf
2 tbsp thyme, chopped
1 parsnip, peeled and thinly sliced
3 tbsp olive oil
3 tbsp chopped flat-leaf parsley, to serve
Salt and freshly ground black pepper

1 Season the game. Heat half the butter in a large frying pan over a medium heat and seal the game. Transfer to the slow cooker and stir in the flour.

2 Heat the remaining butter and soften the onions, carrots, celeriac and turnips over a medium heat. Transfer to the slow cooker. Add the stock, bay leaf and thyme and cook for 4 hours on the high setting or 8 hours on low.

3 Meanwhile, fry the parsnip slices in a frying pan with the oil over a medium heat, until just golden.

4 Serve piping hot with the fried parsnip and scattered with the parsley.

beef with beetroot, parsnips and horseradish cream

In this recipe a usually tough cut of meat becomes meltingly tender through gentle slow cooking, and its flavour is enhanced by the sweetness of the beetroot and parsnips. The horseradish cream is an ideal accompaniment if you want to add a bit of a kick to the dish.

serves **6** • prep time **15 mins** • cooking time **4 hours on high/8 hours on low**

1.4 kg beef stewing steak, diced
2 tbsp oil
30 g butter
2 tbsp plain flour
2 onions, cut into wedges
**350 g beetroot, peeled and
  cut into wedges**
**350 g parsnips, peeled and
  cut into wedges**

1 bay leaf
1 large sprig of thyme
3 tbsp chopped mixed herbs
300 ml hot beef stock
3 tbsp creamed horseradish, to serve
3 tbsp soured cream, to serve
Salt and freshly ground black pepper

1 Season the beef. Heat half the oil and the butter in a large frying pan over a high heat. Cook the beef in batches until well browned. Spoon into the slow cooker and stir in the flour.

2 Heat the remaining butter and oil in the frying pan and brown the onions, beetroot and parsnips. Transfer everything to the slow cooker, add the bay leaf, thyme, mixed herbs and stock and cook for 4 hours on the high setting or 8 hours on low.

3 Meanwhile, mix together the horseradish and soured cream in a small bowl and season well.

4 Serve the beef hot with the horseradish cream and, if you like, some green vegetables of your choice.

rich beef casserole

This is a classic yet simple beef casserole with a silky, hearty sauce that coats the meat and vegetables beautifully, just inviting some warm crusty bread to mop up the juices. If you want to pep up your 5-a-day, serve it with some steamed seasonal green vegetables.

serves **4** • prep time **20 mins** • cooking time **4 hours on high/8 hours on low**

2 tbsp sunflower or olive oil
50 g butter
750 g beef stewing steak, diced
1 tsp cayenne pepper
300 ml hot beef stock
150 g streaky bacon, each rasher
  cut into 3
250 g carrots, peeled and cut into
  large chunks

2 onions, peeled and roughly chopped
1 celery stick, chopped
30 g plain flour
2 bay leaves
2 tbsp thyme leaves
Salt and freshly ground black pepper

1 Heat half the oil and butter in a large frying pan over a high heat. Season the beef and stir in the cayenne pepper. Cook the beef in batches until well browned and spoon into the slow cooker. Pour a little of the stock into the frying pan to deglaze it and use a wooden spoon to scrape off any residue. Transfer to the slow cooker.

2 Heat the remaining oil and butter in the frying pan and brown the bacon, carrots, onions and celery. Transfer to the slow cooker.

3 Stir the flour into the casserole mixture, add the bay leaf, thyme and remaining stock and cook for 4 hours on the high setting or 8 hours on low.

4 Check the seasoning and serve the casserole piping hot.

MEAT-FREE
MEALS

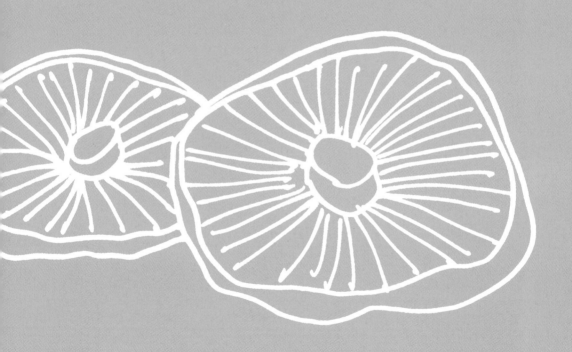

hearty ribollita

Like numerous Italian dishes, ribollita has so many variations that no two bowls of this soup-cum-stew are ever the same. I'd like to say that this is an authentic version, but, to err on the side of caution, I'll say it's inspired by the Tuscan dish. Keep this dish true to its peasant roots by using up whatever vegetables you have spare.

 serves **4-6** • prep time **20 mins** • cooking time **4 hours on high/8 hours on low**

3 tbsp olive oil
2 onions, peeled and diced
2 carrots, diced
3 celery sticks, diced
6 garlic cloves, thinly sliced
3 tbsp freshly chopped rosemary
2 tsp fennel seeds, lightly crushed
Large pinch of chilli flakes
2 bay leaves
400 g can cannellini beans, drained and rinsed
400 g can plum tomatoes, roughly crushed

1 litre hot vegetable stock
125 g stale good-quality bread, such as ciabatta or sourdough, torn into small chunks
250 g cavolo nero or chard thickly sliced (if using cavolo nero, blanch in boiling water for 2 minutes before adding to the pot)
Best-quality extra virgin olive oil, to serve
Salt and freshly ground black pepper

1 Heat the oil in a large frying pan over a medium heat, add the onions, carrots, celery, garlic, rosemary, fennel seeds, chilli flakes and bay leaves and cook for 5 minutes until starting to soften. Transfer to the slow cooker, add the beans, tomatoes, stock, bread and season well. Cook for 4 hours on the high setting or 8 hours on low.

2 About 20 minutes before the end of the cooking time, add the cavolo nero or chard and continue cooking.

3 Serve in large bowls, with a good glug of extra virgin olive oil drizzled over.

classic veggie chilli with zingy avocado salsa

This is the ultimate vegetarian chilli – so packed with flavour that you'll never miss the meat. If you're a chilli lover, serve a small dish of thinly sliced chillies or some pickled jalapeños alongside for that extra kick.

serves **4-6** • prep time **20 mins** • cooking time **4 hours on high/8 hours on low**

3 tbsp olive oil
1 aubergine, cut into 2 cm cubes
1 onion, diced
3 garlic cloves, chopped
1 carrot, diced
1 tbsp mild chilli powder
1 tsp ground cumin
1 tsp ground coriander
2 tbsp tomato purée
2 tsp cocoa powder
1 courgette, diced
2 peppers, diced
100 g green beans, cut into 3 cm lengths

400 g can chopped tomatoes
400 g can red kidney beans, drained
  and rinsed
Pinch of sugar (optional)
Salt and freshly ground black pepper
1 large ripe avocado, peeled, stoned
  and diced
10 cm piece of cucumber, halved,
  seeded and finely diced
Few sprigs of coriander, chopped
Few sprigs of mint, chopped
4 spring onions, thinly sliced
Zest and juice of 1 lime

1 Heat 2 tablespoons of the oil in a large frying pan over a high heat, add the aubergine and fry for 5 minutes, stirring, until browned. Transfer to the slow cooker.

2 Add the remaining oil to the frying pan and fry the onion, garlic, carrot and spices for 5 minutes over a medium heat until slightly softened. Stir in the tomato purée and cook for a further minute before adding the cocoa, courgette, peppers, green beans, tomatoes and kidney beans. Allow to heat through then transfer to the slow cooker. Season well, adding a pinch of sugar (if using) and cook for 4 hours on the high setting or 8 hours on low.

3 While the chilli is cooking, make the salsa by mixing together all the ingredients in a serving bowl. Taste and add a little extra lime juice, if you like. Chill until required. Serve the chilli with some rice, baked potatoes or wedges, with the salsa on the side.

mushroom stroganoff
with green peppercorns and herby rice

This is a deliciously 'meaty' non-meat dish. Buy a good mix of mushrooms for this stroganoff, to give it different shapes and colour. Chestnut mushrooms, large flat, portobellini and button are all widely available and equally tasty.

 serves **4** • prep time **15 mins** • cooking time **4 hours on high/8 hours on low**

2 tbsp olive oil
15 g butter
2 onions, peeled and thinly sliced
3 garlic cloves, peeled and thinly sliced
2 tsp sweet paprika
1½ tsp green peppercorns in brine, drained and roughly crushed
4 tbsp brandy
150 ml hot strong mushroom or vegetable stock

2 medium waxy potatoes, peeled and cut into 2 cm dice
650 g mixed mushrooms, cut into 2 cm thick slices
250 g white rice
Small bunch of flat-leaf parsley, chopped
Handful of celery leaves
142 ml pot soured cream
Salt and freshly ground black pepper

1 Heat the oil and butter in a large frying pan over a medium heat and brown the onions and garlic. Stir in the paprika and peppercorns and cook for a further minute. Carefully add the brandy and bring it to the boil – watch out, it may flare up – then add the hot stock.

2 Place the potatoes and mushrooms in the slow cooker and pour over the onion mixture. Season, then cook for 4 hours on the high setting or 8 hours on low.

3 About 15 minutes before serving, cook the rice according to the packet instructions, drain, and mix with half the parsley and the celery leaves.

4 Season the stroganoff to taste, then add the soured cream and heat through for a few minutes. Stir in the remaining parsley to serve.

rich provençal sauce for pasta

Slow cookers are invaluable when you want to produce a gutsy, slowly reduced tomato sauce. If you are cooking this dish for non-veggies and want to boost the flavour, add six chopped anchovy fillets before cooking. This is delicious served with buttered fresh tagliatelle.

serves **6** • prep time **15 mins** • cooking time **4 hours on high/8 hours on low**

6 tbsp extra virgin olive oil
6 garlic cloves, finely chopped
200 ml red wine
3 tbsp chopped rosemary
1 bay leaf
75 g 'dry' pitted olives, roughly sliced

3 tbsp capers in brine, drained
2 x 400 g cans plum tomatoes,
   roughly crushed
400 g can artichoke hearts,
   drained and sliced
Salt and freshly ground black pepper

1 Heat the oil in a large frying pan over a medium heat, add the garlic and cook for a few minutes until it softens. Pour in the red wine, increase the heat and boil rapidly until the wine has reduced by two-thirds. Add the remaining ingredients to the pan, bring to a simmer and transfer the sauce to the slow cooker.

2 Season well and cook for 4 hours on the high setting or 8 hours on low.

pearl barley, butternut squash and sage risotto

A hugely successful flavour combination, butternut squash and sage has become a popular feature on many a good gastro-pub menu. In this recipe the sweet orange flesh of the squash melts into a rich, nutty, pearl barley risotto.

 serves **6** • prep time **15 mins** • cooking time **3½ hours on high/7 hours on low**

4 tbsp extra virgin olive oil
1 onion, finely chopped
4 garlic cloves, chopped
2 celery sticks, diced
200 ml white wine
3 tbsp chopped sage leaves
1 bay leaf
1 large butternut squash, peeled,

seeded and cut into 3 cm chunks
350 g pearl barley, washed well
1.7 litres hot vegetable stock
75 g finely grated Parmesan or strongly
    flavoured vegetarian cheese
Large knob of butter
Salt and freshly ground black pepper

1 Heat the oil in a large pan over a medium heat and cook the onion, garlic and celery for 5 minutes until slightly softened. Add the wine, increase the heat and boil for a few minutes until reduced by half. Transfer to the slow cooker.

2 Stir in the sage, bay leaf, squash, barley and stock, season well, cover and cook for 3½ hours on the hight setting, 7 hours on low. Stir in the cheese and butter just before serving. If you like a little more bite to your risotto, 3 hours on high, 6 hours on low will be fine.

split pea daal with butter naan

A steaming bowl of chana daal is pure Indian comfort food. It is equally delicious served cold, drizzled with a little olive oil and served with chapati and a crisp salad.

serves **4** • prep time **15 mins, plus soaking** • cooking time **4 hours on high/8 hours on low**

300 g split peas (also called yellow peas or chana daal)
1.2 litres hot vegetable stock
2 tbsp sunflower or olive oil
25 g butter
3 tsp coriander seeds, crushed
1½ tsp cumin seeds, crushed
1 large onion, finely chopped
4 garlic cloves, chopped
1 red and 1 green chilli, thinly sliced

50 g fresh root ginger, peeled and finely chopped
Zest and juice of 1 lemon
25 g coriander, roughly chopped
150 g baby leaf spinach
Salt and freshly ground black pepper
25 g salted butter, at room temperature
Large pinch of chilli powder
1 tbsp finely chopped coriander
2 x 150 g plain cooked naan breads

1 Wash the split peas and leave to soak in cold water for 8 hours, or overnight. Drain and place in a large saucepan, cover with the stock and bring to the boil. Simmer for 15 minutes, skimming off any foam with a spoon, then transfer to the slow cooker.

2 In a large frying pan, heat the oil and butter then add the coriander, cumin, onion, garlic, chillies and ginger and cook for 5 minutes until the onion is soft. Transfer to the slow cooker, season well and cook for 4 hours on the high setting or 8 hours on low.

3 About 5 minutes before the end of cooking, check the seasoning then stir in the lemon zest and juice, fresh coriander and spinach leaves. Allow to heat through.

4 For the naan, preheat the grill to medium. Mix together the butter, chilli powder and coriander. Sprinkle both sides of each naan with water and place them under the grill, bottom-side up, for 2 minutes. Turn, spread with the spiced butter and grill for a further 1–2 minutes until golden and bubbling. Serve straight away with the daal.

thai green curry with pan-fried tofu

Making your own Thai curry paste from scratch requires patience and a lot of ingredients, so you might think it's not worth the efffort; especially when you taste this delicious recipe, whch uses good-quality bought paste!

serves **4** • prep time **15 mins** • cooking time **4 hours on high/8 hours on low**

3 tbsp sunflower or groundnut oil
200 g shallots, peeled and sliced
3 garlic cloves, chopped
3 tbsp good-quality bought Thai green curry paste
2 fresh or dried kaffir lime leaves
1 tsp palm sugar or light muscovado sugar
400 g can coconut milk
150 ml hot vegetable stock
2 tsp Thai fish sauce (omit for vegetarians)

600 g waxy potatoes, peeled and cut into 3 cm chunks
2 carrots, peeled, halved lengthways and cut thickly on the diagonal
2 peppers, roughly chopped
150 g green beans, halved
150 g baby corn
250 g firm tofu, cut into 3 cm cubes
250 g bok choi, leaves separated
3 tbsp roughly chopped coriander
Lime wedges, to serve

1 Heat 2 tablespoons of the oil in a medium frying pan over a high heat, add the shallots and garlic and cook for 5 minutes until golden. Stir in the curry paste, lime leaves and sugar and cook for a minute until aromatic. Pour in the coconut milk, stock and fish sauce (if using) and bring to the boil.

2 Place the potatoes in the slow cooker followed by the carrots, peppers and green beans. Pour over the hot liquid, scatter the corn on top and cook for 4 hours on the high setting or 8 hours on low.

3 About 10 minutes before the end of the cooking time, heat the remaining oil in the frying pan over a high heat, add the tofu and fry until golden. Stir into the curry with the bok choi and coriander and leave for 2 minutes until the leaves have wilted. Serve the curry scattered with coriander and with some lime wedges alongside to squeeze over for a little extra zing!

red pepper falafel bake

If you're anything like me and find sesame-crusted falafel hard to resist, you are sure to love this falafel-inspired loaf. Filled with the classic flavours of cumin, coriander and tahini, it makes a great slow-cooker dish. Serve it warm or chilled with the yoghurty dip and some crisp salad leaves.

serves **4-6** • prep time **25 mins** • cooking time **5 hours on high/10 hours on low**

1 tbsp coriander seeds
2 tsp cumin seeds
465 g jar roasted red peppers in brine, drained
2 x 400 g cans chickpeas, drained
3 garlic cloves, crushed
4 tbsp tahini paste
3 tbsp extra virgin olive oil
Juice of 1 lemon
2 tbsp toasted sesame seeds

50 g fresh white breadcrumbs
100 g spring onions, finely sliced
4 tbsp roughly chopped coriander
Salt and freshly ground black pepper
15 cm piece cucumber, halved and seeded
150 g natural yoghurt
1 tbsp tahini paste
2 tbsp chopped dill
Squeeze of lemon juice

1 Toast the coriander and cumin seeds in a small frying pan over a medium heat until aromatic, then transfer to a pestle and mortar and grind until coarse. Pat the peppers dry on kitchen paper, then cut into 1 cm dice.

2 In a food processor, put three-quarters of the chickpeas, the garlic, tahini, olive oil and lemon juice. Pulse until coarse, then scoop into a bowl and mix in the ground spices with the peppers, sesame seeds, breadcrumbs, spring onions and coriander. Season well.

3 Spoon everything into a well-oiled slow cooker, smooth the surface, scatter with the reserved chickpeas and cook for 5 hours on the high setting or 10 hours on low.

4 For the dip, coarsely grate the cucumber then squeeze out the juice between your hands. Transfer to a bowl and combine with the yoghurt, tahini, dill and some lemon juice to taste. Serve alongside the falafel bake.

porcini mushroom and ale casserole
with thyme dumplings

If you're searching for the ultimate comfort food for the colder months, look no further than a hearty casserole with dumplings. Choose a paler-coloured ale, as darker varieties can be too bitter once cooked, and be sure to buy an extra bottle to serve at the table!

serves **4** • prep time **25 mins, plus 20 minutes soaking** • cooking time **4 hours on high/ 8 hours on low**

15 g dried porcini mushrooms
2 tbsp olive oil
16 shallots, peeled and halved
3 carrots, cut into chunks
3 celery sticks, sliced
25 g butter
350 g chestnut mushrooms, halved
300 ml light ale
2 tbsp fresh chopped thyme
2 bay leaves
1 tbsp wholegrain mustard

3 tbsp mushroom ketchup
300 ml hot mushroom or vegetable stock
2 tsp cornflour
Salt and freshly ground black pepper

For the dumplings
200 g self-raising flour
1 tsp English mustard powder
100 g salted butter, chilled
1 tbsp chopped thyme
1 tbsp finely chopped parsley

1 Place the porcini mushrooms in a bowl, cover with 100 ml boiling water and leave to soak for 20 minutes. Remove the mushrooms, drain briefly and roughly chop. Strain the soaking liquid through a sieve lined with kitchen paper and set aside.

2 Heat the oil over a medium-high heat in a large frying pan, add the shallots, carrots and celery and cook for 5 minutes until tinged brown. Spoon into the slow cooker. Add the butter to the pan, increase the heat, add the porcini and chestnut mushrooms, season well and cook for 5 minutes until golden. Transfer everything to the slow cooker.

3 Pour the ale into the frying pan and boil rapidly for a few minutes until reduced by half. Add the herbs, mustard, mushroom ketchup, stock and the reserved mushroom liquor. Bring to a simmer, and pour into the slow cooker.

4 Mix the cornflour with 2 tablespoons cold water in a small bowl until smooth, then add to the casserole and stir. Cook for 4 hours on the high setting or 8 hours on low.

5 About 40 minutes before the end of the cooking time, make the dumplings. Sieve the flour and mustard into a large bowl and season well. Coarsely grate the cold butter into the flour, dipping it into the flour to prevent sticking. Add the herbs and rub in the butter until the texture resembles coarse breadcrumbs. Add 6–8 tablespoons cold water a tablespoon at a time, mixing with a table knife to combine, until you have a soft, lightly sticky dough. Cut into 8 portions and shape into balls. Drop onto the casserole, cover, and continue to cook for 30 minutes or until the dumplings have a light springiness.

creamy italian white bean and fennel stew

The distinctive aniseed flavour of fennel always makes me think of the Mediterranean and this Italian-inspired dish is no exception. I've added mascarpone to this stew to add a little naughtiness to an otherwise super-healthy dish!

 serves **4** • prep time **20 mins** • cooking time **3 hours on high/6 hours on low**

2 tbsp olive oil
15 g butter
1 large sweet onion, peeled and diced
4 garlic cloves, chopped
2 celery sticks, thinly sliced
400 g turnips, peeled and cut into
   2 cm cubes
3 medium fennel bulbs, cut into large
   wedges, fronds removed and set
   aside for garnish

2 x 400 g cans cannellini or haricot
   beans, drained
75 ml dry vermouth or white wine
2 sprigs of rosemary, leaves only
2 bay leaves
400 ml hot vegetable stock
100 g mascarpone cheese
Crusty bread, to serve
Salt and freshly ground black pepper

1 Heat the oil and butter in a large frying pan and cook the onion, garlic, celery, turnip and fennel wedges until light golden, then transfer to the slow cooker. Add the beans, vermouth, herbs and stock. Season well and cook for 3 hours on the high setting or 6 hours on low.

2 At the end of the cookting time, place the mascarpone in a bowl, spoon in some of the hot cooking liquor and blend until smooth. Pour the mixture into the slow cooker, add the reserved fennel fronds, stir, then serve with crusty bread.

swede, jerusalem artichoke and chestnut hotpot

It's a shame, but Jerusalem artichokes are often overlooked as a winter vegetable. However, once you've tried them in this dish, teamed with rich chestnuts and juicy swede, you'll be digging out the recipe books for other ways to serve them.

serves **4** • prep time **20 mins** • cooking time **4 hours on high/8 hours on low**

25 g butter
1 tbsp sunflower oil
1 onion, sliced
1 leek, sliced into 1cm rounds
2 celery sticks, sliced
1 medium swede, peeled and cut into
   3 cm chunks
500 g Jerusalem artichokes, scrubbed
  well and halved if large

2 tbsp chopped thyme
2 bay leaves
Freshly grated nutmeg, to taste
500 ml hot vegetable stock
200 g vacuum-packed, cooked,
   peeled chestnuts
Salt and freshly ground black pepper

1 Melt the butter and oil in a large frying pan over a medium–high heat, add the onion, leek, celery and swede and fry for about 10 minutes until golden brown. Transfer to the slow cooker with the remaining ingredients.

2 Season well and cook for 4 hours on the high setting or 8 hours on low. Serve with crusty bread.

waldorf loaf

Inspired by the classic salad, this meatloaf-style loaf makes a comforting winter meal served with mashed or roast potatoes and buttered greens, or a satisfying summer dish served cold with crusty bread, a peppery-leaved salad and a glass of chilled white wine.

serves **6** • prep time **20 mins** • cooking time **2 hours on high/5 hours on low**

2 tbsp olive oil
6 shallots, peeled and finely chopped
1 tbsp thyme leaves
4 sprigs of rosemary, leaves finely chopped
100 ml dry white wine
1 large carrot, peeled and coarsely grated
1 eating apple, cored and chopped

2 tsp English mustard powder
1 tbsp sherry vinegar
100 ml hot vegetable stock
200 g walnut pieces
3 celery sticks, cut into small dice
125 g fresh wholemeal breadcrumbs
200 g Stilton or other hard blue cheese, crumbled
Salt and freshly ground black pepper

1 Heat the oil in a large frying pan over a medium heat and cook the shallots, thyme and rosemary until golden. Add the wine and boil rapidly until very little liquid remains. Stir in the carrot, apple and mustard powder and cook for 2 minutes. Pour in the vinegar and stock and heat through.

2 Meanwhile, blend 150 g of the walnuts in a food processor until coarse and tip out into a bowl. Roughly chop the remaining walnuts and add to the bowl along with the celery and breadcrumbs. Mix in the cooked ingredients, season well, then spoon into a well-buttered slow cooker.

3 Cook for 2 hours on the high setting or 5 hours on low. Leave to cool, uncovered, for 15 minutes before serving.

chickpea and paneer curry with cool salsa

Pan-fried paneer (Indian cheese) makes this curry a really substantial yet healthy meal. Paneer is available from most good supermarkets and specialist shops, but if you can't get it, hard-boiled eggs make an equally delicious substitute.

serves **6** • prep time **15 mins** • cooking time **4 hours on high/8 hours on low**

3 tbsp sunflower oil
2 medium onions, thinly sliced
4 garlic cloves, chopped
1 red chilli, finely chopped
6 cardamom pods, seeds only,
   roughly crushed
1 tsp ground turmeric
5 tsp garam masala
2 tsp fennel seeds
1 large potato, about 300 g, peeled
   and diced

2 x 400 g cans chickpeas, drained
500 g pot natural yoghurt
3 tbsp mango chutney
450 g paneer, cut into 3 cm cubes
Salt and freshly ground black pepper
Zest and juice of 2 limes
2 tbsp chopped coriander
2 tbsp chopped mint
3 medium ripe tomatoes, seeded and
   finely chopped
1 shallot, finely chopped

1 Heat 2 tablespoons of the oil in a large frying pan over a medium heat and cook the onions, garlic, chilli and spices until deep golden. Transfer to the slow cooker and stir in the potato, chickpeas, yoghurt and mango chutney.

2 Season well and cook for 4 hours on the high setting or 8 hours on low. Meanwhile, heat the remaining oil in the frying pan, add the paneer and cook for about 5 minutes, stirring often until it turns a deep golden brown. Remove from the pan and set aside, then stir it into the curry 10 minutes before the end of the cooking time.

3 For the salsa, mix together the lime zest and juice, coriander, mint, tomatoes and shallot. Season well and allow to stand at room temperature for an hour to allow the flavours to infuse. Serve alongside the curry.

smoky chipotle black bean chilli tacos

This chilli ticks all the boxes for an informal meal for friends or a speedy family supper. It's cheap and hassle-free to make, rich and smoky, and really healthy too! It's also perfect as a topping for a fluffy baked potato.

serves **4** • prep time **10 minutes** • cooking time **4 hours on high/8 hours on low**

3 tbsp olive oil
1 large red onion, finely chopped
6 garlic cloves, chopped
1 tsp chipotle chilli paste
1 tsp smoked paprika
1 bay leaf
600 g fresh ripe tomatoes, roughly
   chopped

2 x 400 g cans black beans, drained
   and rinsed
3 tbsp chopped coriander
12 taco shells, to serve
200 g soured cream, to serve
200 g medium Cheddar, grated, to serve
Salt and freshly ground black pepper

1 Heat the oil in a large frying pan and fry the onion and garlic for 5 minutes on a medium heat until softened. Add the chilli paste, paprika and bay leaf and cook for a further minute. Stir in the tomatoes, then transfer everything to the slow cooker.

2 Season well, stir in the beans and cook for 4 hours on the high setting or 8 hours on low. Stir through the coriander once cooked.

3 To serve, place the chilli on the table and allow everyone to fill their tacos with chilli and a spoonful of soured cream and cheese. (As an optional extra you could also serve shredded iceberg lettuce and diced cucumber.)

moorish potato and cauliflower stew

In this stew, fragrant and sweet aromatic spices turn two humble vegetables into a really special dish. Crush your potatoes a little on the plate to soak up all the vibrant broth, and use a spoon to scoop up every last tasty drop!

serves **4–6** • prep time **20 mins** • cooking time **3 hours on high/6 hours on low**

3 tbsp olive oil
1 large sweet onion, peeled and
   roughly chopped
2 garlic cloves, sliced
600 g baby (bite-sized) new potatoes,
   scrubbed
2 tsp coriander seeds, ground
2 tbsp tomato purée
5 cm piece cinnamon stick
Large pinch of saffron

1 large celery stick, sliced
1 medium cauliflower, about 500 g,
   broken into florets
75 g sultanas
400 g can butterbeans, drained
700 ml hot vegetable stock
3 large fresh tomatoes, peeled, seeded
   and chopped
40 g flaked almonds, toasted

1 Heat the oil in a large frying pan over a medium heat and cook the onion, garlic and potatoes for 4–5 minutes until tinged brown. Add the coriander seeds and tomato purée and cook for a further minute, stirring.

2 Place the cinnamon, saffron, celery, cauliflower, sultanas and butterbeans in the slow cooker. Stir in the onion and potato mixture and pour over the stock. Check the seasoning then cook for 3 hours on the high setting or 6 hours on low.

3 Before serving, stir through the tomatoes and scatter each individual portion with toasted almonds.

sweet and sour vegetable noodles

If you're put off by the luminous colour of take-away sweet and sour dishes, this easy-to-cook home-made version will be a welcome alternative. The natural flavours of the vegetables are enhanced by zingy citrus tones and delicate spices.

serves **4** • prep time **20 mins** • cooking time **3 hours on high/6 hours on low**

1 tbsp sunflower oil
1 large onion, thickly sliced
100 g cashew nuts
2 carrots, halved lengthways and sliced
   thickly on the diagonal
2 celery sticks, sliced
4 garlic cloves, chopped
30 g fresh root ginger, peeled and cut
   into matchsticks
Pinch of chilli flakes
1 star anise
1 green and 1 red pepper, thickly sliced
225 g can water chestnuts

4 tbsp rice wine vinegar
4 tbsp mirin, rice wine or dry sherry
2 tbsp caster sugar
Juice of 1 lemon
125 ml pineapple juice
2 tbsp cornflour
1 tbsp sesame oil
600 g cooked egg noodles
150 g mangetout, halved
8 spring onions, thinly sliced on the
   diagonal
Salt and freshly ground black pepper

1 Heat the oil in a large frying pan over a high heat and cook the onion for 2 minutes. Add the cashews, carrots, celery, garlic and ginger and cook for a further 2–3 minutes until tinged with brown. Transfer to the slow cooker and scatter over the chilli flakes, star anise, peppers and water chestnuts.

2 In a small bowl, combine the vinegar, mirin or rice wine or sherry, sugar, lemon juice, pineapple juice and cornflour until smooth. Season well and pour the sauce into the slow cooker. Cook for 3 hours on the high setting or 6 hours on low.

3 About 10 minutes before the end of the cooking time, stir in the sesame oil, noodles and mangetout and continue to cook. Serve spooned into bowls and topped with the spring onions.

pardina lentil bolognese

If you want a few simple pasta sauces in your repertoire, this one is sure to become a family favourite. As it cooks your kitchen will fill with a mouthwatering herby, tomatoey aroma that will call everyone to the table without you needing to!

serves **6** • prep time **20 mins** • cooking time **4 hours on high/8 hours on low**

6 tbsp extra virgin olive oil
2 red onions, finely chopped
6 garlic cloves, chopped
1 large carrot, diced
2 celery sticks, diced
2 courgettes, diced
100 g tomato purée
2 x 400 g cans chopped tomatoes

200 g pardina lentils
300 ml vegetable stock
2 bay leaves
40 g basil, roughly chopped
1½ tsp dried oregano
1 tbsp thick balsamic vinegar
1 tsp granulated or caster sugar
Salt and freshly ground black pepper

1   Heat the oil in a large frying pan over a medium heat, then add the vegetables and cook for 5 minutes until lightly softened, but not coloured. Add the tomato purée and cook for 2 minutes. Add all the remaining ingredients, reserving about a third of the basil, season well, and bring to a simmer.

2   Transfer to the slow cooker and cook for 4 hours on the high setting or 8 hours on low. Stir through the remaining basil before serving with your favourite pasta, or use the sauce to make a delicious lasagne.

COOKING
FOR FRIENDS

creamy chicken and mushroom

If you're entertaining friends midweek, you want a recipe that's simple to cook, welcoming, and suits all tastes. This is the perfect dish for sharing; delicately flavoured, creamy and inviting, it will get everyone talking.

serves **6** • prep time **15 mins** • cooking time **4 hours on high/8 hours on low**

2 tbsp sunflower or olive oil
30 g butter
2 onions, chopped
2 carrots, peeled and chopped
500 g boneless, skinless chicken
   thighs, diced
2 tbsp plain flour
2 tsp garlic salt
300 ml hot chicken stock

300 ml milk
1 bay leaf
2 large sprigs of thyme
300 g mushrooms, larger ones
   quartered
Salt and freshly ground black pepper
250 g long grain rice, to serve
3 tbsp chopped flat-leaf parsley,
   to serve

1   Heat half the oil and butter in a large frying pan over a medium heat and cook the onions and carrots for 2 minutes. Transfer to the slow cooker.

2   Heat the remaining oil in the frying pan over a high heat and cook the chicken until it is sealed all over. Spoon the chicken into the slow cooker and stir in the flour and garlic salt. Pour over the stock and milk and some black pepper. Add the bay leaf and thyme and cook for 4 hours on the high setting or 8 hours on low.

3   About 15 minutes before the end of the cooking time, cook the rice according to the packet instructions and stir the mushrooms into the chicken. Garnish with the parsley and serve hot over the rice.

chicken tikka masala

This perennial favourite works very well in the slow cooker. Set it to cook before you head off to work on Friday morning and you can return home to restorative curry with pickles, poppadums and cold beer.

serves **6** • prep time **20 mins** • cooking time **4 hours on high/8 hours on low**

1.5 kg chicken pieces
2 tbsp oil
2 onions, chopped
120 ml coconut milk
400 g can chopped tomatoes
120 ml natural low-fat yoghurt
1 tsp cornflour
3 tbsp tomato purée
1 tbsp cumin seeds
2 tsp garam masala
1 tbsp black onion seeds
5 cm piece of fresh root ginger,

chopped
3 tbsp freshly squeezed lemon juice
2 garlic cloves, chopped
2 tsp cayenne pepper, or to taste
1 red chilli, chopped
15 g mint, chopped
15 g coriander, chopped
Lime wedges, to serve
350 g basmati rice, to serve
Naan bread, to serve
Raita, to serve

1   Heat the oil in a large frying pan over a high heat and brown the chicken pieces all over. Transfer to the slow cooker.

2   Heat the remaining oil in the frying pan over a high heat and cook the onions for 5 minutes. Set aside. Add the coconut milk and tomatoes to the slow cooker. Mix the yoghurt with the cornflour and stir this in too.

3   Using a blender or food processor, blend the fried onion with the rest of the ingredients up to and including the chilli. Add to the slow cooker and cook for 4 hours on the high setting or 8 hours on low.

4   Just before serving, cook the rice according to the packet instructions. Stir the mint and coriander into the curry and serve hot with the rice, naan bread and some raita on the side.

chicken tagine

with baby aubergines, coriander and sumac

Baby aubergines are easy to find in ethnic stores and some supermarkets and are well worth searching out, as their mild heat and pepperiness adds a lot of flavour to dishes. Sumac is a spice mix that is becoming increasingly popular and available – look out for it in the supermarket or deli.

serves **6** • prep time **15 mins** • cooking time **4 hours on high/8 hours on low**

1.5 kg chicken pieces
4 tbsp olive oil
2 onions, chopped
2 carrots, chopped
5 baby aubergines, halved
2 garlic cloves, left whole
1 cinnamon stick
1 bay leaf

1 tbsp sumac powder
1 lemon, sliced
200 ml hot chicken stock
400g can chopped tomatoes
400 g couscous, to serve
30 g coriander, chopped to serve
Natural yoghurt, to serve
Salt and freshly ground black pepper

1 Season the chicken. Heat the oil in a large frying pan over a medium heat and cook the chicken until golden. Transfer to the slow cooker.

2 Heat the remaining oil in the frying pan over a medium heat and brown the onions, carrots, aubergines and garlic. Stir in the cinnamon, bay leaf, sumac, lemon, stock and tomatoes. Transfer to the slow cooker and cook for 4 hours on the high setting or 8 hours on low.

3 Just before serving, prepare the couscous according to the packet instructions. Stir the coriander into the tagine and serve hot over the couscous with the natural yoghurt in a small serving bowl.

tandoori chicken

Another Indian classic; I think this is just as nice cold for a casual weekend lunch, with a bit of salad and fresh bread, as it is served hot with the traditional accompaniments. The ultimate mood food!

serves **6** • prep time **10 mins** • cooking time **4 hours on high/8 hours on low**

50 g butter	1 lemon, chopped
1 tbsp cayenne pepper	1 red onion, chopped
2 garlic cloves, crushed	Coriander, to garnish
1 tbsp garam masala	Lemon wedges, to serve
1 tbsp coriander seeds, crushed	Raita, to serve
1 onion, finely chopped	Naan bread, to serve
2 kg chicken	Salt and freshly ground black pepper

1 Use a pestle and mortar or a food processor to blend together the butter, cayenne, garlic, garam masala, coriander seeds, onion and seasoning.

2 Take the chicken and pat dry with kitchen paper. Use a small sharp knife to make slashes in the breast, thigh and drumsticks. Rub the spice paste into the chicken, pushing well into the flesh where you have cut it with the knife.

3 Put the lemon and red onion in the base of the slow cooker and set the chicken on top. Cover and cook for 4 hours on the high setting or 8 hours on low.

4 Serve hot or cold with the lemon wedges, raita and naan bread on the side.

Note: Suitable for a 6 litre model; for the 3 litre size, use a 1.2 kg chicken

jalapeño chicken with tacos

I think of this as match food – if the football is on, or any other sporting competition – this is perfect fodder for excited fans. Lay it out on a table and get your friends to help themselves before they settle in front of the tv.

serves **6** • prep time **15 mins** • cooking time **4 hours on high/8 hours on low**

3 tbsp olive oil
2 red onions, chopped
2 green peppers, chopped
4 garlic cloves, chopped
3 tbsp tomato purée
1 tsp paprika
2 tsp ground cinnamon
1 tbsp coriander seeds, crushed
50 g jalapeño chillies, chopped

1 tsp fresh lemon juice
400 g can blackeye beans, drained
1.5 kg chicken pieces
1 tbsp plain flour
Iceberg lettuce, chopped, to serve
Guacamole, to serve
Taco shells, to serve
Salt and freshly ground black pepper

1 In the slow cooker, mix half the oil with the onions, peppers, garlic, tomato purée, paprika, cinnamon, coriander seeds, chillies, lemon juice, beans and seasoning.

2 Heat the remaining oil in a large frying pan over a medium heat and fry the chicken until golden all over. Season well and stir in the flour. Spoon into the slow cooker and cook for 4 hours on the high setting or 8 hours on low.

3 Serve the chicken hot with the iceberg lettuce and guacamole for stuffing into the tacos.

slow-roast duck with apples

The simple flavours in this dish are rich and intensely satisfying, and the fruity combination of apple and orange is a great success. It's a real taste of the English countryside; ideal for a lazy lunch or dinner after an autumnal walk.

serves **6** • prep time **15 mins** • cooking time **4 hours on high/8 hours on low**

6 duck legs, excess fat removed
2 tbsp plain flour
250 ml cider
1 tbsp olive oil
2 carrots, chopped
400 g shallots, peeled
Zest pared in one piece from 1 orange

300 ml hot chicken stock
4 tbsp chopped thyme
450 g Granny Smith apples, chopped
12 tbsp cider vinegar
Salt and freshly ground black pepper
80 g watercress, to garnish

1 Season the duck legs and fry in a large, dry frying pan over a high heat. Drain on kitchen paper then put in the slow cooker. Stir in the flour.

2 Deglaze the frying pan with the cider and pour the liquid into the slow cooker.

3 Heat the oil in the frying pan over a medium heat and cook the carrots and shallots for a few minutes until golden. Add to the slow cooker with the orange zest, stock, thyme, apples and cider vinegar. Cook for 4 hours on the high setting or 8 hours on low.

4 Serve garnished with watercress.

lamb biryani

An aromatic, mild curry; the fragrant flavours in the sauce gently pervade the rice. Using brown rice makes the dish extra healthy, and basmati is ideal for those who are not keen on plain brown, as it has a more subtle texture.

serves **6** • prep time **15 mins** • cooking time **3 hours on high/6 hours on low**

6 tbsp vegetable or sunflower oil
1 kg lamb shoulder, diced
2 onions, chopped
3 garlic cloves, chopped
5 cm piece of fresh root ginger, chopped
1 bay leaf
2 tsp coriander seeds, crushed
2 tsp cumin seeds
1 tsp chilli flakes

200 g brown basmati rice, washed
2 tbsp tomato purée
100 ml coconut milk
100 ml natural yoghurt
300 ml hot lamb stock
25 g mint, chopped
25 g coriander, chopped
6 spring onions, finely sliced
Mango chutney, to serve
Salt and freshly ground black pepper

1 Heat half the oil in a frying pan over a high heat and brown the lamb. Season well and transfer to the slow cooker.

2 Heat the remaining oil in the frying pan over a medium heat and fry the onions, garlic, ginger, bay leaf, coriander seeds, cumin seeds, and chilli flakes for 2 minutes until the spices are aromatic and the onion is softened. Mix in the rice, transfer to the slow cooker and stir in the tomato purée.

3 Pour over the coconut milk, yoghurt and stock and cook for 3 hours on the high setting or 6 hours on low.

4 Just before serving, combine the mint, coriander and spring onions and sprinkle the mix over the biryani. Offer the mango chutney alongside for guests to help themselves to.

lamb and lentil curry

This is a lovely, easy, hearty curry that will create a warm glow around the table. The addition of lentils means you need less meat, which makes this dish easy on the purse, too.

serves **6** • prep time **15 mins** • cooking time **4 hours on high/8 hours on low**

1.2 kg lamb, diced
2 tbsp oil
2 onions, chopped
4 garlic cloves, crushed
5 cm piece of fresh root ginger, finely grated
1 tbsp crushed dried chillies
1 tsp fennel seeds (optional)
1 tbsp coriander seeds

1 tbsp cumin seeds
100 g green lentils
500 ml hot lamb stock
500 g tomato passata
1 bay leaf
4 tbsp roughly chopped coriander, to serve
Cooked basmati rice, to serve
Salt and freshly ground black pepper

1 Season the lamb. Heat half the oil in a large frying pan over a high heat and brown the lamb well all over. Transfer to the slow cooker.

2 Heat the remaining oil in the frying pan and cook the onions, garlic and ginger over a medium heat for 5 minutes until softened. Stir in the bay leaf, chillies, fennel (if using), coriander and cumin seeds and season well. Transfer everything to the slow cooker and add the lentils, stock and passata. Cook for 4 hours on the high setting or 8 hours on low.

3 Serve hot, garnished with the fresh coriander and accompanied by the rice.

greek-style lamb with feta and parsley

This is one of my favourite recipes; the potatoes magically absorb the full flavour of the lamb, and the feta adds a deliciously contrasting texture and taste to the dish. Perfect for a lazy Sunday lunch in the summer sun.

serves **6** • prep time **15 mins** • cooking time **4 hours on high/8 hours on low**

1 kg lamb shoulder, diced
3 tbsp chopped rosemary
2 onions, quartered
1 head garlic, cut in half horizontally
4 tomatoes, halved
500 g waxy potatoes, peeled and
   thickly sliced
100 ml white wine

200 ml hot chicken stock
100 ml olive oil
200 g feta cheese, crumbled
50 g flat-leaf parsley, roughly chopped
Grated zest and juice of 1 lemon
5 tbsp olive oil
Salt and freshly ground black pepper

1 Season the lamb. Put the rosemary, onions, garlic, tomatoes and potatoes in the slow cooker and place the lamb on top.

2 Pour over the wine, hot stock and 100 ml oil and cook for 4 hours on the high setting or 8 hours on low.

3 Combine the feta cheese, parsley, lemon zest and juice and olive oil and stir through the lamb just before serving.

lamb and pea curry

Peas are a great addition to a curry, as they provide fresh flavour and bump up the vegetable content – and I always seem to have a bag of peas in the freezer! This simple dish needs no more than some warm naan bread to mop up the juices, Indian pickles, such as lime or aubergine, and a cool raita to accompany it.

serves **6** • prep time **20 mins** • cooking time **4 hours on high/8 hours on low**

1.2 kg minced lamb
2 tbsp oil
2 onions, chopped
2 garlic cloves, crushed

3 tbsp medium curry powder
300 ml hot lamb stock
300 g tomato passata

1 Season the lamb. Heat half the oil in a large frying pan over a high heat and brown the lamb well. Transfer to the slow cooker.

2 Heat the remaining oil in the frying pan over a medium heat and cook the onions and garlic for about 2 minutes until softened. Stir in the curry powder. Transfer the pan contents to the slow cooker, add the stock and passata and cook for 4 hours on the high setting or 8 hours on low.

3 Serve hot, with your preferred accompaniments.

braised pork with caramelised leeks

Pork and leek is a combination that never fails; the sweetness of leeks perfectly enhances the flavour of pork. In this recipe, the juices of the braised meat are transformed into a rich sauce with the addition of a little double cream.

serves **4** • prep time **20 mins** • cooking time **4 hours on high/8 hours on low**

1 kg pork shoulder, diced
4 tbsp olive oil
2 onions, chopped
2 carrots, chopped
4 garlic cloves, chopped
3 tbsp thyme leaves, chopped
1 bay leaf
100 ml hot chicken stock

200 ml cider
100 ml double cream
30 g butter, to serve
2 leeks, finely sliced, to serve
2 tbsp demerara sugar, to serve
Mashed potato, to serve
Sea salt and freshly ground
  black pepper

1 Season the pork. Heat half the oil in a frying pan over a high heat and brown the pork on all sides. Spoon into the slow cooker.

2 Heat the remaining oil in the frying pan over a medium heat and soften the onions, carrots and garlic. Spoon into the slow cooker.

3 Add the thyme, bay leaf, stock, cider and cream. Mix well, season and cook for 4 hours on the high setting or 8 hours on low.

4 About 10 minutes before serving, heat the butter in a frying pan over a medium heat and cook the leeks, stirring often, until really soft and golden. Stir in the sugar and, when melted, remove from the heat.

5 Serve the pork, garnished with the leeks, over mashed potato.

slow-roasted chinese-style pork ribs

If you love Chinese food but are put off making it because of the lists of ingredients or variety of dishes on offer, try this simple recipe. The mellow and sweet flavours of the Chinese ingredients tease out the rich flavours of the pork, and through long slow cooking they all meld together in a rich and piquant sauce. Once you've tried this, you won't rush for the Chinese take-away menu again!

serves **6** • prep time **15 mins** • cooking time **4 hours on high/8 hours on low**

4 tbsp finely grated fresh root ginger	1.5 kg pork spare ribs
3 garlic cloves, crushed	1 tbsp sesame oil
1 tbsp chilli flakes (optional)	300 g cooked long grain rice, to serve
200 ml hoisin sauce	3 eggs, beaten, to serve
4 tbsp clear honey	2 spring onions, chopped, to serve
50 ml rice wine or mirin	

1 Combine the ginger, garlic, chilli flakes (if using) hoisin sauce, honey and rice wine in a large bowl. Add the pork and mix until the sauce coats the spare ribs evenly. Add everything to the slow cooker and cook for 4 hours on the high setting or 8 hours on low.

2 About 5 minutes before the end of the cooking time, heat the sesame oil over a high heat in a wok or large frying pan and add the cooked rice. Stir and toss for 2 minutes, until the rice is heated through, then add the beaten egg and spring onions and stir until combined.

3 Serve the spare ribs with the sauce poured over and accompanied by the egg-fried rice.

beef in tomato and basil

Basil is available in supermarkets throughout the year, but is best in summer, when it is in season; this is when its flavour is strongest and its aniseed notes, which complement the strong flavours of the beef, most pronounced.

serves **6** • prep time **15 mins** • cooking time **4 hours on high/8 hours on low**

800 g stewing steak or shin of beef, diced
4 tbsp olive oil
2 onions, diced
2 carrots, diced
2 rosemary sprigs, leaves only
4 garlic cloves
200 ml Italian red wine

200 ml hot beef stock
2 tbsp tomato purée
500 g tomato passata
Pinch of sugar
4 tbsp basil leaves, torn
Extra virgin olive oil, to serve
Pasta of your choice
Parmesan shavings, to serve

1 Season the beef. Heat half the oil in a large frying pan over a high heat and cook the beef until well browned all over. Spoon into the slow cooker.

2 Heat the remaining oil in a frying pan over a medium heat and brown the onions and carrots. Chop the rosemary and garlic together, so that the flavours combine, and stir into the pan. Pour on the wine, let it bubble a bit, then transfer everything to the slow cooker.

3 Add the stock, tomato purée, passata and sugar then cook for 4 hours on the high setting or 8 hours on low.

4 Just before serving, cook the pasta according to the packet instructions and stir the basil and a glug of oil through the beef.

5 Serve hot with pasta and pass around the Parmesan separately.

spicy beef with chipotle sauce and coriander

Mexican food is perfect for sharing with friends at an informal supper, not least because it can be stretched to include unexpected guests by adding accompaniments. This is a lovely Tex-Mex dish bursting with colour, flavour and texture. Rinsing the chillies gives the sauce a nice rounded heat without that sense of burning.

serves **6** • prep time **15 mins** • cooking time **4 hours on high/8 hours on low**

2 tbsp olive or sunflower oil
1.4 kg stewing steak, diced
1 carrot, roughly diced
2 green peppers, roughly diced
3 red onions, roughly chopped
3 garlic cloves, crushed
100 ml hot beef stock
4 tbsp tomato purée
3 tbsp mild chilli powder

2 tbsp chilli flakes
3 spring onions, chopped
$^1/_2$ cucumber, peeled, seeded
  and diced
100 g natural yoghurt
50 g soured cream
Handful of coriander leaves, to serve
250 g long grain rice, to serve
Salt and freshly ground black pepper

1 Heat 1 tablespoon of oil in a large frying pan over a high heat and cook the beef until well browned. Transfer to the slow cooker.

2 Add the remaining oil to the frying pand and cook the carrot, green peppers and onions for a few minutes until softened. Add to the slow cooker with the garlic, stock, tomato purée and chilli powder. Season well and cook for 4 hours on the high setting or 8 hours on low.

3 Combine all the chilli sauce ingredients in a bowl and set aside until ready to eat.

4 Just before serving, cook the rice according to the packet instructions. Serve the spicy beef over the rice, scattered with coriander and accompanied by the chilli sauce.

Note: Suitable for the 3 litre model, the recipe can be doubled for larger models

meatball cassserole with tomato sauce

Meatballs are always popular, enjoyed by young and old alike, and this is a delicious way of allowing all the lovely flavours to develop in a rich sauce. I don't always use egg when forming meatballs, but they need it when cooked in a slow cooker, otherwise they will fall apart.

serves **6** • prep time **20 mins** • cooking time **4 hours on high/8 hours on low**

400 g minced beef
400 g minced pork
1 egg, beaten
4 tbsp olive oil
1 onion, chopped
2 carrots, chopped
3 garlic cloves, chopped
1 celery stalk, chopped

1 tbsp tomato purée
100 ml red wine
2 x 400 g cans chopped tomatoes
1 tbsp mixed herbs
1 tsp sugar
Sea salt and freshly ground
  black pepper

1 Mix together the beef, pork, egg and seasoning in a large bowl. Divide the mixture into 12 and shape each piece into a meatball. They don't have to be perfect, but try to get them as compact as you can.

2 Heat half the oil in a large frying pan over a high heat and seal the meatballs, cooking them until golden brown all over. Transfer to the slow cooker.

3 Heat the remaining oil in the frying pan and cook the onion, carrots, garlic and celery for 5 minutes until softened. Transfer to the slow cooker. Stir in the tomato purée, red wine, chopped tomatoes, mixed herbs, sugar and seasoning. Cook for 4 hours on the high setting or 8 hours on low.

4 Serve hot, with pasta, if you wish.

steak and ale casserole

This is a warm-hearted and welcoming stew, perfect when the weather outside is chilly and uninviting! It is also one of the most rewarding recipes to cook in a slow cooker. The firm stewing steak gradually breaks down over lengthy cooking to produce a velvety textured sauce and succulent meat.

serves **6** • prep time **15 mins** • cooking time **4 hours on high/8 hours on low**

1.4 kg stewing steak, diced
50 g butter or sunflower spread
2 tbsp plain flour
300 ml hot beef stock
1 bay leaf
1 large sprig of thyme
3 onions, diced

3 carrots, diced
2 celery stalks, diced
200 ml ale or beer
1 tsp English mustard
4 tbsp chopped curly parsley
Seasonal green vegetables, to serve

1 Season the beef. Heat half the butter or sunflower spead in a large frying pan over a high heat and cook the beef in batches until well browned. Spoon into the slow cooker and stir in the flour.

2 Pour a little of the stock into the frying pan and use a wooden spoon to scrape off any residue. Transfer to the slow cooker with the bay leaf and thyme. Heat the remaining butter or sunflower spread and cook the onions, carrots and celery over a medium heat until softened. Add to the slow cooker with the remaining stock, the beer and mustard. Stir well.

3 Cook for 4 hours on the high setting or 8 hours on low.

4 Serve hot with green vegetables of your choice.

veal stew with polenta

Veal shoulder becomes beautifully tender and moist in a slow cooker. In this dish the wine releases all its aromas into the braising liquid as the stew gently cooks, so make sure you use a good-quality white wine that has a significant but not overpowering flavour.

serves **6** • prep time **10 mins** • cooking time **4 hours on high/8 hours on low**

1 kg veal shoulder, diced
4 tbsp olive oil
1 tbsp flour
2 turnips, diced
2 onions, diced
2 celery stalks, diced
1 bay leaf
2 sprigs thyme leaves

200 ml hot chicken stock
200 ml white wine
250 g quick-cook polenta, to serve
2 tbsp extra virgin olive oil, to serve
4 tbsp finely chopped flat-leaf parsley
Sea salt and freshly ground
   black pepper

1 Season the meat. Heat half the oil in a large frying pan over a high heat and brown the veal. Transfer to the slow cooker and stir in the flour.

2 Heat the remaining oil in the frying pan over a high heat and cook the turnips, onions and celery for 5 minutes until softened. Transfer to the slow cooker.

3 Stir in the bay leaf, thyme, stock and white wine. Season well and cook for 4 hours on the high setting or 8 hours on low.

4 About 10 minutes before serving, cook the polenta according to the packet instructions and stir through some seasoning and the extra virgin olive oil.

5 Serve the veal stew spooned over the polenta, and garnished with the parsley.

slow-cooked rabbit with parsley and garlic

One of the joys of slow cooking is to transform tough cuts of meat into melt-in-the-mouth dishes through tender loving cooking. To discourage intensive farming, we should make an effort to vary the kinds of meats that we eat. Try cooking rabbit in the slow cooker, and be ready to put it on your shopping list more often. Rabbit needs a rich sauce, and in this recipe the lashings of olive oil bring the flavours of the naturally lean rabbit to life.

 serves **4** • prep time **15 mins** • cooking time **4 hours on high/8 hours on low**

1 kg rabbit pieces, or 1 whole rabbit, jointed
4 tbsp olive oil
150 g pancetta, diced
4 garlic cloves, crushed
2 onions, chopped
2 carrots, diced
100 ml white wine
100 ml hot chicken stock
1 bay leaf
15 g flat-leaf parsley, chopped
Salt and freshly ground black pepper
500 g gnocchi, to serve

1 Season the rabbit. Heat half the oil in a large frying pan over a high heat and brown the rabbit and pancetta well. Transfer to the slow cooker.

2 Heat the remaining oil in the frying pan over a medium heat and soften the garlic, onions and carrots. Transfer to the slow cooker.

3 Deglaze the pan with the wine, and add to the slow cooker with the stock and bay leaf. Season well and cook for 4 hours on the high setting or 8 hours on low.

4 Just before serving, cook the gnocchi according to the packet instructions. Stir the parsley into the rabbit sauce and serve hot, spooned over the drained gnocchi.

WEEKEND
POT ROASTS

garlic and herb-stuffed chicken

This is a dish for all seasons – it is delicious served hot in the colder months with fresh crusty bread for mopping up the juices, but it also lends itself perfectly to the summer, served cold with a crisp green salad and seasonal new potatoes.

serves **6** • prep time **15 mins** • cooking time **4 hours on high/8 hours on low**

100 g butter
2 tbsp chopped flat-leaf parsley
2 tbsp chopped thyme
3 garlic cloves, crushed

2 kg chicken
100 ml white wine (optional)
Salt and freshly ground black pepper

1 Mash together the butter, herbs, garlic and seasoning. Take the skin of the chicken breast at the thickest part and pull it away from the meat. Using your fingertips, push the garlic and herb butter in between the skin and breast, as far along as you can, so that the whole chicken gets basted. Be careful towards the centre of the breast, as the skin is thin here and can tear easily.

2 Set the chicken in the slow cooker and pour the wine into the bottom. Cover and cook for 4 hours on the high setting or 8 hours on low.

3 Remove the chicken from the cooker. Serve hot with the buttery juices spooned over or cold, simply sliced, depending on your preference!

Note: Suitable for 6 litre model; for the 3 litre size, use a 1.2 kg chicken

butter-basted whole chicken
with lemon and thyme

When chicken is cooked this way, it is succulent and full of flavour remaining moist even when cooked. Try serving it at room temperature in the warmer months with a crunchy selection of summer vegetables.

serves **8** • prep time **10 mins** • cooking time **4 hours on high/8 hours on low**

50 g butter
Juice and zest of 1 lemon
2 tbsp thyme leaves
1 x 2 kg chicken
150 ml chicken stock
3 tbsp cornflour

2 tbsp chopped parsley (optional)
Salt and freshly ground black pepper
Sugar snap peas, to serve
Baby carrots, to serve
Mangetout, to serve

1 Mash together the butter, lemon juice and zest, thyme and salt and pepper. Using your fingerts, push the butter in between the skin and breast of the chicken or rub it all over the chicken breast.

2 Place the chicken in the slow cooker and pour the stock into the bottom. Cover and cook for 4 hours on the high setting or 8 hours on low.

3 Remove chicken from the cooker and set aside to keep warm while you make the sauce.

4 To make the sauce, spoon off the excess fat from the cooking liquid and place the remaining juices in a pan over a medium heat. Mix the cornflour in a cup with a little water and then stir into the gravy together with the parsley, if using, and bring to a simmer to thicken. Simmer for 3–4 minutes, to cook the cornflour and allow the flavours to mellow, before serving with the chicken and vegetables.

rice-stuffed shoulder of lamb

Lamb is the ideal meat for a slow-cooked pot roast, as it becomes succulent and releases all its flavour. You will get the best flavour if you brown the lamb before adding it to the slow cooker, but if time does not allow, it will still turn golden during cooking. If you can't get shoulder, a boned leg of lamb also works well in this recipe.

serves **6** • prep time **15 mins** • cooking time **4 hours on high/8 hours on low**

1 kg shoulder of lamb, boned
2 tbsp olive oil
2 garlic cloves, sliced
1 lemon, roughly chopped
100 g easy-cook or
   parboiled white rice, cooked

10 sun-dried tomatoes, halved
100 ml white wine
500 g waxy potatoes, cut into large dice
Salt and freshly ground black pepper
You will need 2 metal skewers

1   Season the lamb all over. Heat the oil in a large frying pan over a high heat, and brown the lamb on the outside. (This can be tricky, as the lamb will not be a neat shape.)

2   Remove from the heat and leave the lamb in the pan. In the larger muscles at either end of the joint, make a deep incision to divide the piece into two. Insert some of the garlic and lemon in these deep incisions, and tuck the rest into the remaining meat. Spoon over half of the rice, pushing it into the incisions, and add the sun-dried tomatoes. Now fold the joint in two, with the opening uppermost, and secure with the metal skewers. Spoon over the remaining rice, pushing it into the opening. Push as much of the filling that has fallen out back into the opening. Transfer the lamb to the slow cooker.

3   Return the frying pan to the heat and add the wine to the pan juices. Heat until just sizzling then pour the pan contents over the lamb. Add the potatoes to the slow cooker, season well, and cook for 4 hours on the high setting or 8 hours on low.

4   Serve the lamb and the rice together, with the diced potatoes.

herby garlic-roasted lamb

Long slow cooking gently tenderises this premium lamb joint, and it tastes particularly good with garlic, as the flavours blend together and become milder. A real taste of the Mediterranean for a lazy weekend lunch in the sun.

serves **6** • prep time **15 mins** • cooking time **4 hours on high/8 hours on low**

1 kg leg of lamb	¹⁄₂ lemon, chopped
2 tbsp olive oil	100 ml white wine
1 garlic head	1 kg potatoes, peeled and halved
15 g flat-leaf parsley	Salt and freshly ground black pepper
15 g thyme	

1 Season the lamb all over. Heat the oil in a large frying pan over a high heat and brown the lamb on the outside. (This can be tricky, as the lamb will not be a neat shape.)

2 Slice the garlic in half horizontally and place the pieces in the slow cooker. Chop together the herbs with some seasoning and add to the slow cooker. Add the lemon and pour over the wine.

3 Transfer the lamb to the slow cooker and cook for 4 hours on the high setting or 8 hours on low.

4 When cooked, remove the lamb using a carving fork and strain the juices left behind in the slow cooker through a sieve into a jug. Spoon off any excess fat in the juices and check the seasoning.

5 Serve the lamb and juices together, with simple potatoes.

slow-roasted pork belly with star anise

This is a delicate, Chinese-spiced dish that will melt in the mouth after lengthy cooking. However, if you prefer more texture, cook this ahead of time then remove the pork belly slices and roast them for 20 minutes at 220°C/gas 7 just before serving so that they crisp up; then serve them separately to the broth.

serves **6** • prep time **15 mins** • cooking time **4 hours on high/8 hours on low**

2 tbsp sesame oil
1.5 kg boneless belly of pork, rind removed
6 spring onions, left whole
3 carrots, roughly chopped
2 garlic cloves, chopped

4 star anise
100 ml hot chicken stock
100 ml rice wine
3 heads pak choi, quartered
Rice noodles, cooked to serve

1 Heat the oil in a large frying pan over a high heat. Add the pork and cook for 5 minutes, turning often, until browned. Transfer to the slow cooker.

2 Add the remaining ingredients to the slow cooker and cook for 4 hours on the high setting or 8 hours on low.

3 About 5 minutes before the end of cooking time, add the pak choi and stir through.

4 Serve the broth and the pak choi in bowls with the rice noodles and with the pork belly on a separate serving dish.

sesame-roasted pork shoulder

Sweet roasted sesame seeds are fantastic with pork, adding a depth of flavour to the meat and the sauce. Serve it with plain long grain rice and steamed vegetables, such as broccoli, to offset the richness of the dish.

serves **6** • prep time **20 mins** • cooking time **4 hours on high/8 hours on low**

1 tbsp sunflower oil	**100 ml hot chicken stock**
2 carrots, diced	**50 g clear honey**
1 red onion, diced	**100 g sesame seeds**
1.3 kg pork shoulder joint, skin removed	**2 tsp English mustard powder**
3 garlic cloves, peeled	**Salt and freshly ground black pepper**

1 Heat the oil in a large frying pan over a high heat and cook the carrots and onion for 3 minutes or so until just softened. Spoon into the slow cooker.

2 Season the pork joint and brown it all over in the same pan, without oil. Transfer to the slow cooker with the garlic, stock, honey and seasoning.

3 In a dry pan over a medium heat, roast the sesame seeds until aromatic. Scatter them over the pork joint and cook for 4 hours on the high setting or 8 hours on low.

4 To serve, remove the pork and strain the sauce in the slow cooker into a pan. Boil the sauce for 5 minutes to reduce.

5 Slice the pork, and serve with the sauce and rice or vegetables.

mustard-crusted roast beef with parsnips

This is a classic Sunday lunch in one pot, using the traditional English flavours that complement beef: strong English mustard and hearty sweet parsnips. If you're going all out for the full 'roast' lunch, serve this with creamy mashed potatoes and steamed green cabbage.

serves **6** • prep time **30 minutes** • cooking time **4 hours on high/8 hours on low**

3 tbsp English mustard powder
3 tbsp soft light brown sugar
1.3 kg beef topside or brisket joint
4 tbsp olive oil
2 onions, peeled and cut into wedges
100 ml hot beef stock

2 tbsp chopped thyme leaves
4 parsnips, peeled and halved
  lengthways
2 tbsp cornflour, made into a paste with
  a little cold water
Salt and freshly ground black pepper

1 Mix together the mustard powder and sugar and season well. Press the paste into the fat on the beef joint.

2 Heat half the oil in a large frying pan over a high heat and brown the onions for 5 minutes. Transfer to the slow cooker.

3 Heat the remaining oil in the frying pan over a high heat and cook the beef until well browned. Transfer to the slow cooker. Pour a little of the stock into the frying pan and use a wooden spoon to scrape off any residue, then add to the slow cooker.

4 Add the parsnips to the slow cooker, arranging them around the edge, then cook for 4 hours on the high setting or 8 hours on low.

5 Lift out the beef and parsnips using a carving fork and a slotted spoon onto a serving dish and cover while you make the gravy. Sieve the juices in the slow cooker into a pan. Bring the liquid to a simmer, stir in the cornflour paste and simmer for 2 minutes to thicken slightly. Check the seasoning.

6 Serve the beef and gravy with vegetables of your choice.

pot-roasted beef

with rosemary, thyme and anchovies

Slowly pot-roasting a beef joint allows the meat juices to soak into the potatoes, infusing them with flavour and leaving the beef beautifully succulent and tender. This is a truly wonderful one-pot winter warmer.

serves **6** • prep time **30 minutes** • cooking time **4 hours on high/8 hours on low**

4 tbsp olive oil
1.3 kg beef topside or brisket joint
200 ml hot beef stock
100 ml red wine
2 onions, peeled and roughly chopped
25 g anchovies in olive oil

25 g rosemary leaves
15 g thyme leaves
750 g waxy potatoes, peeled and thickly
   sliced
Freshly ground black pepper

1 Heat half the oil in a large frying pan over a high heat. Season the beef with a little pepper and cook it for about 10 minutes until well browned on all sides. Set aside to cool. Pour a little of the stock into the frying pan and use a wooden spoon to scrape off any residue. Transfer the liquid to the slow cooker along with the wine.

2 Heat the remaining oil in the frying pan and brown the onions. Transfer to the slow cooker.

3 Chop together the anchovies, rosemary and thyme and stuff this mixture into the beef. Place the beef in the slow cooker.

4 Put the potatoes around the beef joint and cook for 4 hours on the high setting or 8 hours on low.

piquant teriyaki pot-roasted beef

This simple beef dish makes a light and slightly spicy alternative to a roast. Serve with steamed green leaves, such as pak choi, to complement the Eastern flavours.

serves **6** • prep time **15 mins** • cooking time **4 hours on high/8 hours on low**

6 spring onions
3 carrots, peeled
1 red pepper, seeded
1.4 kg beef brisket joint
2 tbsp sunflower oil

150 ml teriyaki marinade
Egg noodles, to serve
3 tbsp coriander leaves
3 tbsp finely chopped chives
Salt and freshly ground black pepper

1   Cut the spring onions in half, then cut the carrots in half lengthways, and then half again. Cut the pepper into similar-sized strips. Put all the vegetables into the slow cooker.

2   Season the beef. Heat the oil in a large frying pan over a high heat and brown the beef. Transfer it to the slow cooker, pour over the teriyaki marinade and cook for 4 hours on the high setting or 8 hours on low. Keep basting as often as possible.

3   About 10 minutes before the end of cooking, cook the noodles according to the packet instructions.

4   Slice the beef and serve witht he onions, carrots and pepper. Garnish the beef teriyaki with the coriander and chives, and serve piping hot with the sauce spooned over the noodles.

PUDDINGS

individual caramelised pear and mascarpone cheesecakes

The cleverest thing about this scrumptious dessert is that the base can be used with any other topping, not just the caramelised pear that I have recommended here; try fresh raspberries with granola, or chopped peaches doused in Italian vin santo wine.

serves **6** • prep time **10 mins** • cooking time **4 hours on high/8 hours on low**

120 g digestive biscuits	2 large eggs, beaten
50 g butter, melted	30 g butter, to serve
300 g mascarpone cheese	3 small firm pears, to serve
100 g caster sugar	30 g demerara sugar, to serve
1 tsp vanilla extract	You will need 6 x 150 ml ramekins

1 First, crush the biscuits. The easiest way to do this is to place the biscuits in a strong food bag and crush them with a rolling pin.

2 Mix the crumbs with the melted butter and press the mixture into the ramekins, smoothing the surface with a spoon.

3 Whisk together the mascarpone, sugar, vanilla and eggs in a large bowl until the mixture is smooth, then divide the mix between the ramekins. Cover each dish with foil. Put 3–4 layers of greaseproof paper in the base of the slow cooker and put the covered ramekins on top, stacking if necessary. Pour in hot water to a depth of about 2 cm, cover, and cook for 4 hours on the high setting or 8 hours on low. Allow to cool.

4 To serve, melt the butter in a large frying pan over a medium heat. Peel, core and either slice or chop the pears and add them to the pan. Sprinkle them with the sugar and cook for 5 minutes, or until the sugar is dissolved. Spoon the pears onto the cheesecakes and serve.

tiramisu sponge desserts

This is a great make-ahead dessert – and in fact it tastes better if you allow some time for setting it aside for the flavours to develop. For those who do not like coffee, simply leave it out of the topping.

serves **6** • prep time **10 mins** • cooking time **4 hours on high/8 hours on low**

100 g caster sugar
100 g butter
2 eggs, beaten
50 g grated chocolate
25 g cocoa powder, sieved,
   plus extra to decorate

75 g self-raising flour
250 g mascarpone cheese
2 tbsp icing sugar, sifted
3 tbsp liquid coffee, i.e. Camp
1 tsp vanilla extract
You will need 6 x 150 ml ramekins

1 Beat the sugar and butter together until creamy and smooth, then beat in the eggs slowly, until smooth. Add the chocolate and stir in the cocoa powder. Lastly, stir in the flour.

2 Divide the mixture between the ramekins. Put 3–4 layers of greaseproof paper in the base of the slow cooker and put the ramekins on top, stacking if necessary. Pour in hot water to a depth of about 2 cm and cook for 4 hours on the high setting or 8 hours on low. Allow to cool.

3 To serve, beat together the mascarpone, icing sugar, liquid coffee and vanilla extract until smooth. Spoon a little of this mixture over the top of each chocolate base, sieve over some cocoa powder and serve.

butterscotch rice pudding

Butterscotch is a flavour that takes me straight back to childhood –
in my case to those 'just-add-milk' mousse desserts that my mum would
whip up out of a packet. Delicious as they were to me then, with my
slightly more sophisticated adult tastes, this home-made butterscotch
beats those hands down for flavour.

serves **6** • prep time **20 mins** • cooking time **4 hours on high/8 hours on low**

120 g soft light brown sugar
50 g golden syrup
50 g butter

130 g pudding rice
1.2 litres full-fat milk

1 Mix together the sugar and golden syrup in a pan over a medium heat
and cook for about 5 minutes until the sugar is dissolved. Add the butter and
stir until smooth.

2 Pour the mixture into the slow cooker with the milk and, lastly, stir in the rice.

3 Cook for 4 hours on the high setting or 8 hours on low.

almond and passion fruit bake

Do not serve this dessert to friends and expect to have leftovers. It is a real treat – rich, a little decadent, but divine. All you need with it is some single cream and perhaps a little lie down on the sofa afterwards!

serves **6** • prep time **15 mins** • cooking time **4 hours on high/8 hours on low**

150 g butter
100 g light brown soft sugar
? tsp almond extract
3 eggs, beaten
150 g self-raising flour
100 g ground almonds

100 ml passion fruit juice
50 g caster sugar
2 fresh passion fruit, to serve
You will need 6 x 150 ml ramekins,
   or a 1 litre pudding basin

1 Beat the butter together with the sugar until pale and creamy. Add the almond extract.

2 Beat in the eggs, one at a time, then fold in the flour and stir in the ground almonds. Divide the mixture between the ramekins or place in the pudding basin.

3 Cover the ramekins or pudding basin with foil. If you are using a single pudding bowl you will need a strap made from a length of foil, folded over a few times for strength, that runs underneath the bowl to make it easier to lift out of the slow cooker at the end. Place the ramekin or bowl into the slow cooker, stacking if necessary, and pour in boiling water to a depth of 1–2 cm. Cook for 4 hours on the high setting or 8 hours on low.

4 Meanwhile, in a pan over a medium heat, stir together the pasion fruit juice and sugar until the sugar is dissolved. When the pudding is cooked, remove from the slow cooker, skewer the surface all over and spoon over the syrup, allowing it to drain down into the pudding. Serve warm with a few pieces of passion fruit spooned over each dessert.

toffee and pecan pudding

This pairing of flavours is a perennial favourite. If you want to vary the basic recipe you could try adding a pinch of ground ginger to the mix.

serves **8** • prep time **20 mins** • cooking time **4 hours on high/8 hours on low**

200 g pitted dates
1 tsp bicarbonate of soda
1 tbsp golden syrup
120 g light muscovado sugar
300 g softened butter, plus extra
 for greasing

100 g pecans, roughly chopped
175 g soft dark brown sugar
2 eggs
175 g self-raising flour
Single cream, to serve

1 Put the dates in a saucepan, cover with water and bring to the boil. Add the bicarbonate of soda, which breaks down the skin of the dates and tenderises them, making them easier to digest, and simmer for 5 minutes. Drain well and set aside.

2 To make the sticky toffee sauce, place the syrup, light muscovado sugar and 120 g of the butter in a clean pan and simmer over a gentle heat, together for about 10 minutes, until dissolved. Meanwhile, grease six 150 ml ramekins or a 1 litre pudding bowl that fits your slow cooker. Divide the pecans among the ramekins or place in the pudding bowl. Spoon a little sauce into the prepared bowl(s).

3 For the sponge, beat together the remaining butter, the dark brown sugar, eggs and flour until creamy. Stir the dates into the mixture.

4 Pour the sponge mix into the ramekins or bowl and cover with foil. If using a pudding bowl, you will also need a 'strap' made from a length of foil, folded over a few times for strength, that goes under the bowl to make it easier to lift out of the slow cooker.

5 Put the dishes into the slow cooker, stacking them if necessary. Pour in boiling water to a depth of 1–2 cm, but not more than halfway up the sides of the ramekins. Cook for 4 hours on the high setting or 8 hours on low. Serve warm with single cream.

Index